LOS ANGELES REVIEW OF BOOKS

NO. 22 QUARTERLY JOUR[...] OCCULT

COVER ART: REZA SHAFAHI

front: UNTITLED, 2015, COLORED PENCIL & MARKER ON PAPER, 35.5 X 36.5 CENTIMETERS

The Los Angeles Review of Books is a 501(c)(3) nonprofit organization. The *LARB Quarterly Journal* is published quarterly by the Los Angeles Review of Books, 6671 Sunset Blvd., Suite 1521, Los Angeles, CA 90028. Submissions for the *Journal* can be emailed to EDITORIAL@LAREVIEWOFBOOKS.ORG. Visit our website at WWW.LAREVIEWOFBOOKS.ORG.

The *LARB Quarterly Journal* is a premium of the LARB Membership Program. Annual subscriptions are available. Go to WWW.LAREVIEWOFBOOKS.ORG/MEMBERSHIP for more information or email MEMBERSHIP@LAREVIEWOFBOOKS.ORG.

Distribution through Publishers Group West. If you are a retailer and would like to order the *LARB Quarterly Journal*, call 800-788-3123 or email orderentry@perseusbooks.com.

To place an ad in the *LARB Quarterly Journal*, email ADSALES@LAREVIEWOFBOOKS.ORG.

CONTENTS

NO. 22 QUARTERLY JOURNAL: OCCULT

essays

fiction

poetry

hybrid

shorts

POWER AND CARE

TOWARD BALANCE FOR OUR
COMMON FUTURE—SCIENCE,
SOCIETY, AND SPIRITUALITY

edited by
Tania Singer and Matthieu Ricard
with Kate Karius

with contributions by
His Holiness the Dalai Lama

Transformative Books for Transformative Times

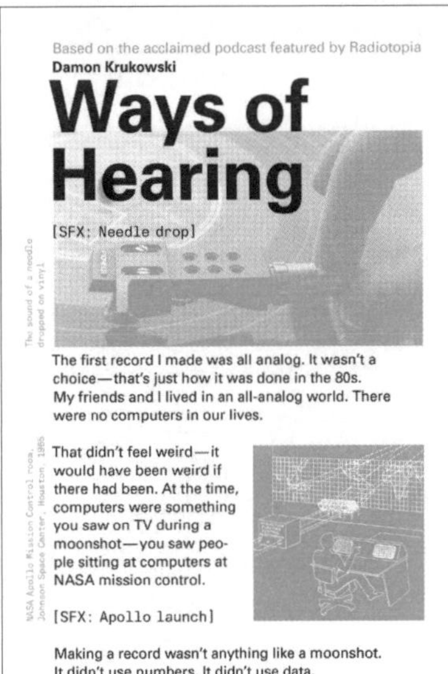

How Change Happens

By Cass R. Sunstein

The different ways that social change happens, from unleashing to nudging to social cascades.

Power and Care

Toward Balance for Our Common Future—Science, Society, and Spirituality

Edited by Tania Singer, Matthieu Ricard and Kate Karius

Leading thinkers from a range of disciplines discuss the compatibility of power and care, in conversation with the Dalai Lama.

Ways of Hearing

By Damon Krukowski

Foreword by Emily Thompson

A writer-musician examines how the switch from analog to digital audio is changing our perceptions of time, space, love, money, and power.

Publishing Manifestos

An International Anthology from Artists and Writers

Edited by Michalis Pichler

Manifestos by artists, authors, editors, publishers, designers, zinesters explore publishing as artistic practice.

Learn more at mitpress.mit.edu/larb

LETTER FROM THE EDITOR

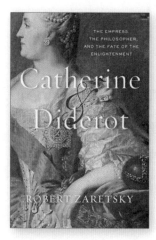

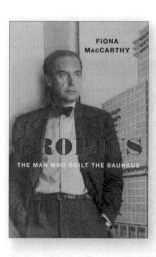

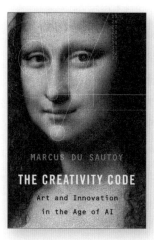

Dear Reader,

I'll start with a ghost story. When I was about nine years old, I traveled to Scotland with an uncle of mine and his family. We stayed in an old hotel, and on that first night I had a dream in which I was wandering around a basement. A disembodied voice told me that I would meet "him" in three days. The next night, I fell asleep and again found myself wandering the same empty basement. The voice said I would now meet "him" in two days. This happened again the following night. Finally, on the fourth night of our stay, I fell asleep, and this time, I found myself in the same basement but in a laundry room. My aunt was pregnant at the time, and she was in the dream, folding clean laundry. I started to help her but realized that there was a pair of gray doors behind me, one opened and one closed. The voice then said that I would meet him tonight and I realized that the "him", whoever he was, was behind the closed door and would soon step into the open doorway. Just before he did, I forced myself to wake up. There was a man, who was also not quite a man, standing at the hotel room window. It was more of a force in the shape of a man but still clearly visible. Long blonde hair, dark purple jacket. I looked around the room – everything was as it had been. I looked between the man and my cousin, who was lying in the bed next to me. I kept looking at her, trying to will her awake, though of course, that didn't work at all. The man approached my bed, and I, in a total panic, hid myself under the covers. I must have fallen asleep. Everything was fine in the morning.

I tell this story not to insist on any truth or reality, but to think about the occult as a subject and as a mode of storytelling. It can really splinter an audience in a way that almost no other subject can. The occult raises issues around belief, as well as the systems that we think govern the universe. It walks the line between the possible and the impossible, the genuine and the feigned, the authentic and the phony. The occult pushes us to accept that different worlds can exist within or beside one another. Indeed, that maybe our world isn't quite what we thought it was. The occult can be a way of challenging our accepted forms of knowledge, both of ourselves and our surroundings.

This issue of the *Los Angeles Review of Books Quarterly Journal* is dedicated to exploring these dynamics. Colin Dickey writes about the Satanic Panic in the 1980s, when parents were convinced that daycare centers were performing satanic rituals on their children. Emily Ogden writes about Charles Durant, a 19th-century balloonist who set out to debunk clairvoyants, examining the thin line between belief and doubt. Paul La Farge writes a short story about a professor and his ghost Anna, connecting the occult to a long history of race relations. Fernando A. Flores imagines a border ruled by corrupt possums, who keep getting book deals.

The occult, or what is categorized as the occult, can be a tool to reexamine what is a real. It's a fun house mirror – disordered and unusual, and yet, still somehow accurate.

Medaya
Editor

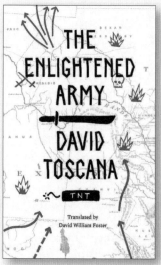

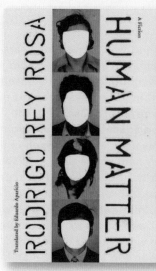

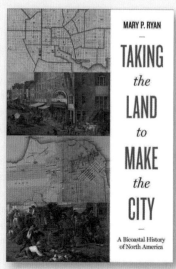

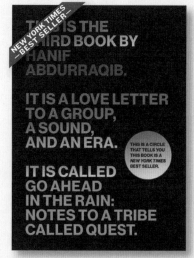

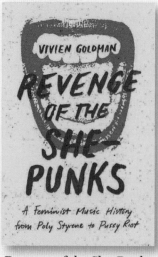

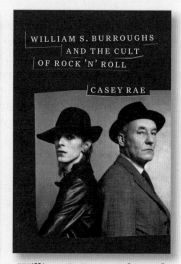

"Each sentence, tight and beautiful, reads like a proof of what powerful fiction can do. And the humor—my god!—when was the last time I laughed so unashamedly while reading a book?"

—Samrat Upadhyay, author of *Mad Country*

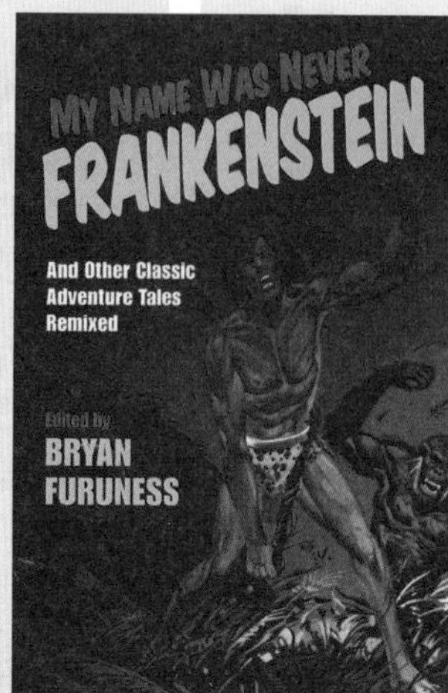

My Name Was Never Frankenstein reanimates your favorite literary characters into new and exciting escapades.

"[N'Sondé's] writing captures the rhythm of a brutal reality of a society on the brink of collective disintegration while simultaneously providing a space for daydreaming."

—*L'Humanité*

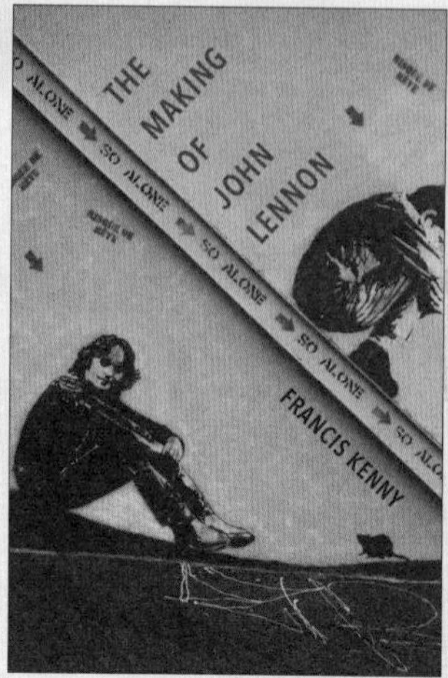

"Focuses on the question of what might have caused the downfall of one of the most brilliant musicians of the past century."

—*Huffington Post*

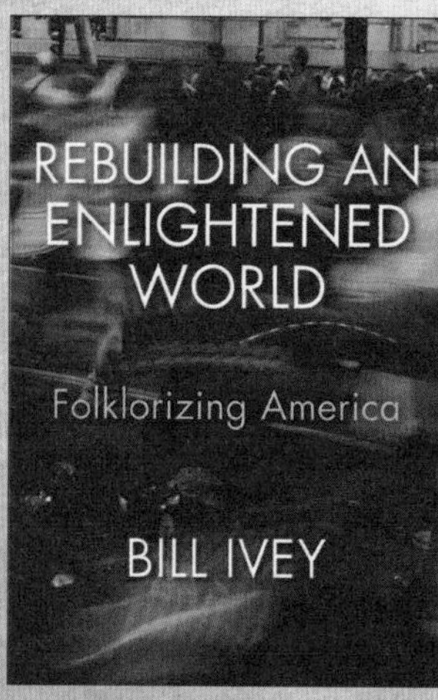

"Ivey's powerful book lays out a path for drawing upon our traditions, customs, and rich cultural heritage to help forge a brighter future—for our own country, and for people across the globe."

—Neera Tanden, President and CEO, Center for American Progress

Featuring exquisite color photographs, *The Life and Art of Felrath Hines* explores the life, work, and artistic significance of Felrath Hines, one of the most noteworthy art conservators of the 20th century.

"A book for our time that is right on time."

—*Journal of Folklore Research*

Balancing intimate memories of playmates and neighborhood crushes with harrowing stories of extremism and authoritarianism, Bagila Bukharbayeva gives a voice to victims in Uzbekistan whose stories would never otherwise be heard.

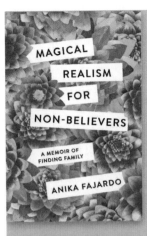

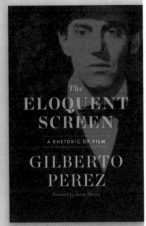

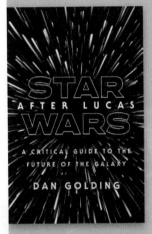

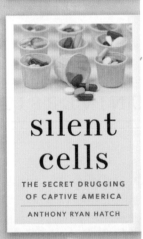

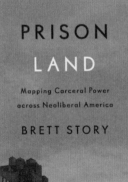

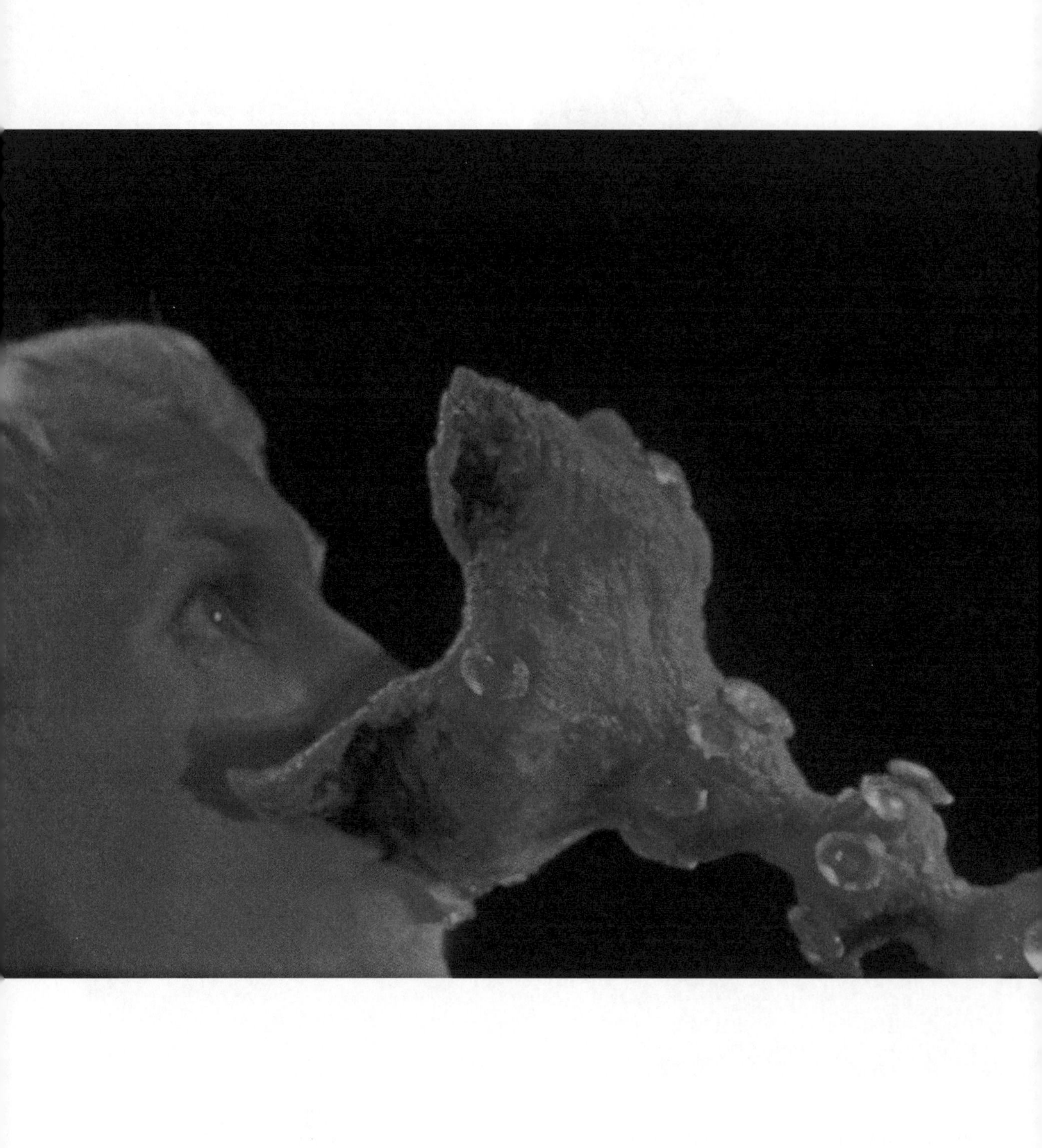

Opposite: Kenneth Anger, *Inauguration of the Pleasure Dome,* 1954-2014. C-Print, 26 × 35 inches. Edition of 7.

Above: Kenneth Anger, *Scarlet Woman (Marjorie Cameron)*, 1954-66. C-Print, 33 1/2 × 45 7/8 inches. Edition of 7.

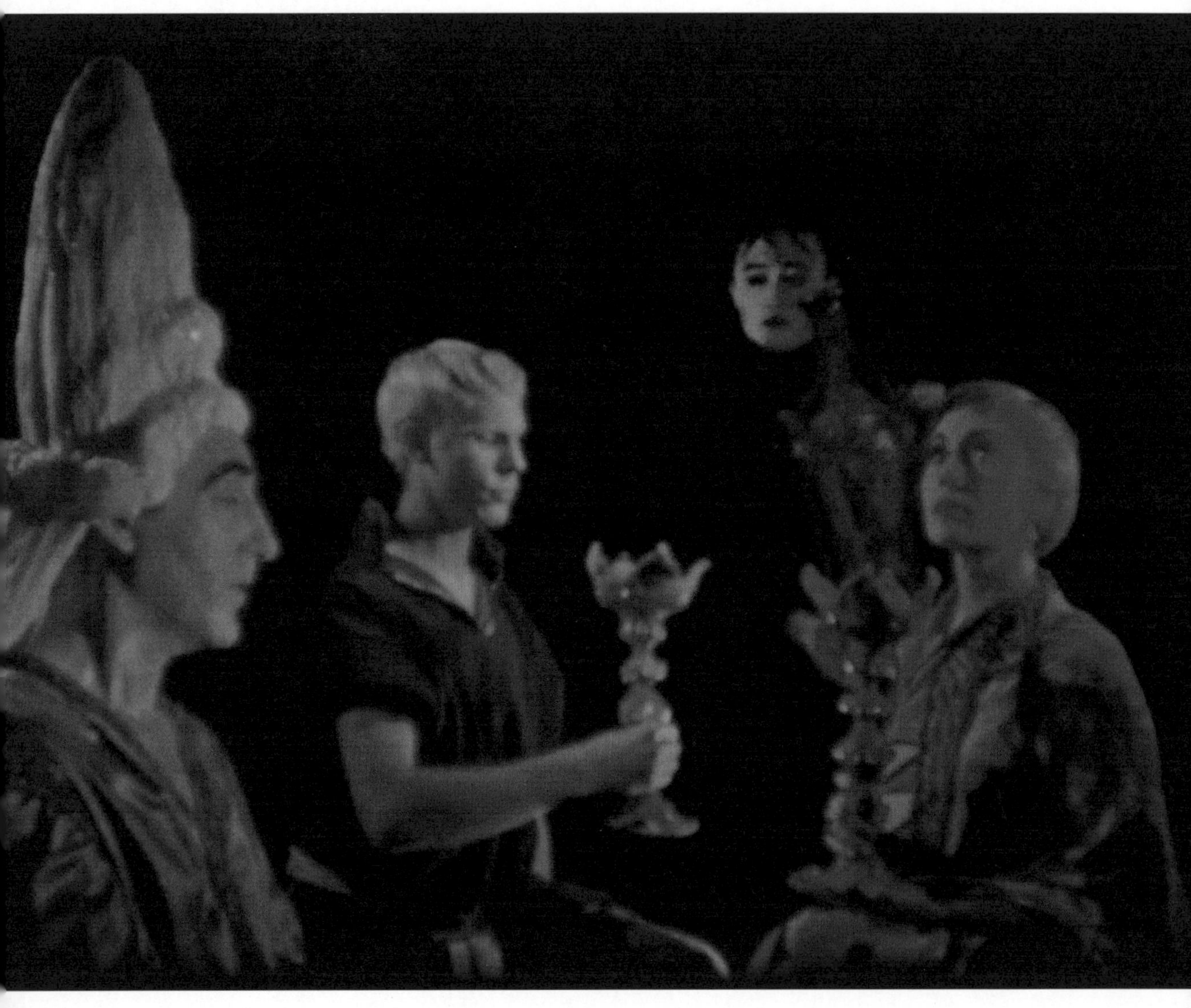

Kenneth Anger, *Inauguration of the Pleasure Dome,* 1954-2014. C-Print, 26 × 35 inches. Edition of 7.

THE SUBURBAN UNCANNY

COLIN DICKEY

Even though Freud popularized the term, he never outright defined what he meant by "the uncanny." He offered instead, a number of examples that might trigger the feeling, including "[t]he factor of the repetition of the same thing," an experience that evokes for him "the sense of helplessness experienced in some dream-states." Freud describes walking through the deserted streets of a provincial town in Italy, getting lost and attempting to find his way, only to arrive again and again at the same street, the twisting narrow streets inevitably returning him to the same place. Getting lost in a forest or mountain fog, and returning to the same spot repeatedly, or feeling about in a dark room and stumbling into the same piece of furniture — these all, Freud suggests, evoke "the same feeling of helplessness and of uncanniness."

Freud was writing before the rise of the suburbs, but in their layout and construction they seemed almost purpose-built to evoke the uncanny. Anyone who's ever been lost in a labyrinth of cul-de-sacs knows this sensation: the houses, row after row of them, the streets seemingly straight but also strangely curved and bent, as if to subtly guide you toward a dead-end in the subdivision's heart. All the houses structurally the same, but with slight variations — perhaps because of a different car in the driveway, a different conglomeration of yard waste at the curb, a distinct rose bush or hedge — eliciting a simultaneous sense of sameness and difference. At night, driving slowly through such a maze, the orange glow of streetlights brightening and fading along the way, or even in daytime, as you pass by house after house shut up against the world, you are in the landscape of disquiet.

Perhaps it was not a question of if, but when, the topography of such spaces would become the locus of a nationwide nightmare.

ꙮ

In 1984, in Manhattan Beach, California, the owners of a respected and elite daycare center, the McMartin Pre-School, were arrested under suspicion of child molestation. A woman named Judy Johnson had accused the staff of molesting her son Matthew, launching a trial that would consume much of the 1980s. The case would become one of the longest and most sensationalized legal battles in American history, and would come to stand in for a whole series of occult conspiracies and allegations about daycare workers that swept through the country like a virus.

This series of legal battles came to be known as the Satanic Panic, which is still associated with daycares because of the McMartin case. All over the country, childcare providers were accused of not just molesting children, but forcing them to participate in increasingly fantastical and elaborate Satanic rituals, involving animal and human sacrifice; orgies and sexual abuse; and brainwashing and memory wipes. And yet, much of the paranoia centered not around businesses but private, suburban homes. Before the McMartin case even broke in Southern California, Bakersfield to the north had been incubating suspicion and fear. In 1982, a woman named Mary Ann Barbour began to suspect that her two granddaughters were being molested by a relative, Rod Phelps. She filed child endangerment charges against their parents and moved to have her daughter-in-law's daycare shut down. Under questioning, the two young girls told authorities they had been abused not only by Phelps, but also by their father. Eventually, they would claim their parents had run a sex trafficking ring, suspended them from hooks while abusing them, and shown them snuff films to warn them what would happen if they ever talked. When police came to search their homes, they found no pornography, or any evidence of hooks, or any other physical evidence to corroborate the children's stories. In what would become a strange hallmark of the child abuse cases to come, children would repeatedly claim they had been subjected to atrocities and abuse for which no forensic evidence could be found, and which often contradicted known facts. The girls' parents were sentenced to over two hundred years each, and would spend the next 12 years in prison until their convictions were finally thrown out.

ꙮ

For decades, it was the city that had been seen as a place of crime and danger, where no one was safe, where no self-respecting middle-class person would venture. The suburbs were the answer: they embodied the locus of the ideal family, middle-class respectability, the signal that one had "arrived," financially and socially. Not coincidentally, they are a place of aesthetic control and conformity, of homeowners associations dictating the color of a house, the height of a tree, the state of a lawn. Aesthetic conformity guarantees property values and ensures kind of cultural homogeneity as well. In response to that outward uniformity, the nuclear family of the suburbs turns inward: the home becomes a private space, its insides are what makes it unique and give it personality.

You can't drive slowly down an avenue of identical houses without giving some thought to how each might be different on the inside. But as fear of secret Satanic cults overtook the nation, that curiosity about what was going on behind those walls became pathological. The stories children told were of a separate suburban landscape, one that seemed to exist alongside this picture of normality, a nightmare world of hidden suburban depravity, laid like a palimpsest over ordinary America. The low-slung houses lining these cul-de-sacs might look identical, each one home to some happy family going about its days — but behind Venetian blinds and locked doors strange rituals were afoot.

Soon the suburban house was defined by what came out of the children's testimonies, testimonies that bore no relation to empirical reality. It was a panic dependent on the construction of fantastical and impossible architecture — a house with endless hidden spaces, always opening up on to some other den of horror, one completely invisible to authorities.

ꕥ

Among those swept up in the Bakersfield panics were Mary and Brad Nokes. Their 10-year-old son Mike was removed from their custody in 1984 and questioned as to whether he'd been abused. At first Mike denied having been molested, then changed his mind six days later, but then reversed his story once more three weeks after that.

When Mike Nokes was asked why he had accused his parents of molestation if it wasn't true, he responded that he had been coached by the county childcare investigator, Cory Taylor. "When I tell the truth," Mike told a private investigator working on behalf of his parents, "she [Taylor] says, 'C'mon. Better start telling me the truth, or I'll keep you in this room all day.'" Subjected to this kind of intense questioning, in which the only correct answer was one that implicated parents and daycare workers, Mike Nokes became hysterical. Alone and subject to the increasing stress of endless questioning, Mike seemed driven by separation anxiety: when the police told his grandparents they could no longer visit him, he accused his grandparents of molestation. When Cory Taylor was taken off the case, he accused her of molestation, too.

Under the intense questioning of another social worker, Carolyn Heims, Nokes finally began telling a story that would send the child abuse panic into a new level of sensationalism. Nokes told Heims not only that he had been abused, but that he had been forced to witness and participate in the ritual murder of infants. "Michael said that once everybody got there, all of the adults would take their clothes off and stand in a square around the children, who were in a circle," reports of his testimony reported. "Michael said that all during this time the adults were chanting prayers to Satan. Michael said that he (and a little girl) were handed knives." Michael said he and the girl were forced to throw their knives at one of the infants, after which "all of the adults started throwing knives that they had."

Nokes's story was so bizarre it seemed impossible that anyone could believe him. Instead, he was not only believed, but Kern County officials began dragging local lakes, searching for evidence of the disposed baby corpses. None were found, though that didn't stop them from believing that this sexual abuse was in fact the work of a secret ring of Satanists.

Nokes and several other children eventually named 27 different victims of this supposed Satanic cult; when it turned out that two people on the list were still alive, and a third had died during surgery, officials were undeterred; they assumed instead that the children had been brainwashed and instructed to recount false memories to throw authorities off the trail of the true story.

What had started as molestation accusations became increasingly baroque, bound up in occult ritual. Judy Johnson, the accuser at the heart of the McMartin case, began leaving increasingly bizarre answering machine messages for the L.A. County investigators, relating her son Matthew's stories of a "goatman," accusing daycare worker, Peggy McMartin, of power-drilling "a child under the arms, armpits." The preschool's atmosphere, she alleged, was one of ritual magic: "Peggy, Babs and Betty were all dressed up as witches. The person who buried Matthew is Miss Betty. There were no holes in the coffin." Bob Currie, a parent of one of the McMartin children who devoted his life to ferreting out Satanic ritual abuse, would later state on *Geraldo*:

> When the children started talking, they started talking about robes and candles. They described an Episcopal church. And once they started narrowing that down, you could see it had to be Satanic. It's very important in Satanic religions to have a priest, because they truly do believe in power. [...] The truth about Satanism is they truly do use blood, and they mix it with urine, and then they also use the real meat, the real flesh. This is what makes Satanism true, and this is what 1,200 molested kids in the city of Manhattan Beach have told the sheriff's department.

ജ്ഞ

What's noteworthy about the Satanic ritual abuse panic of the 1980s was how quickly it became about more than just child abuse. History is rife with sexual abuse scandals orchestrated by large conspiracies — Cardinal Bernard Law resigned from his position as the Archbishop of Boston after documents were unearthed alleging that he had reassigned known abusive priests to different parishes to avoid detection, and the *Miami Herald* has recently detailed how prosecutors have shielded millionaire Jeffrey Epstein from damaging sexual trafficking allegations. But what happened in the 1980s was that the public — and prosecutors — became far more fixated on the suburban occult aspects then the actual abuse. After the McMartin trial ended in a hung jury, nine of 11 jurors held a press conference in which several jurors stated they felt abuse had occurred but hadn't been proven, and that the focus on bizarre stories of animal mutilation, blood drinking, and other occult behavior had tainted those allegations that seemed substantial.

"I am concerned," FBI profiler Ted Lanning would later write, that in some cases "individuals are getting away with molesting children because we cannot prove they are satanic devil worshipers who engage in brainwashing, human sacrifice, and cannibalism as part of a large conspiracy." These fantasies of the occult were something the mind could fixate on, precisely because such cults were hidden, while also being everywhere. And the mere specter of such a terror endured because it responded to so many different aspects of culture all at once.

Why did so many families become convinced of these massive cults, their tentacles reaching throughout the country? For some parents, dealing with either real or imagined guilt that their children may have been victims of abuse, it offered a strange means of assuaging that guilt. As Lanning put it, "If your child's molestation was perpetrated by a sophisticated satanic cult, there is nothing you could have done to prevent it and therefore no reason to feel any guilt." Lanning recalled parents describing day care centers whose cults "had sensors in the road, lookouts in the air, and informers everywhere," a secret, indefatigable network of malevolence that no parent could match.

But Thomas Beck also notes that such fantasies could be empowering, and that they "lent a sort of heroic glow to the very idea of parenting." The middle-class suburbs of the 1980s had become a place of selfishness and lacking in any kind of moral or ethical center. McMartin, Beck notes, "reimagined life there as a battle to preserve that peaceful, comfortable way of life." The Satanic Panic turned the suburbs into a battlefield between Good and Evil, and allowed ordinary parents starring roles in waging Holy War.

ࣙ

In his assessment of the Satanic Panic scare, sociologist Jeffrey S. Victor diagnosed the epidemic as the result of a convergence of forces: when multiple, distinct social groups — each with its own concerns and agendas — begin to fixate on the same topic, the groundswell of concern can grow exponentially as each group echoes and amplifies the others' fears and anxieties. Numerous interest groups also had a stake in fueling the panic, interest groups that had little in common with one another, but made common cause against this nebulous network of occultists and abusers.

Fundamentalist Christians saw accounts of these rituals as proof of the literal work of the Devil, as well as validation that the messages they perceived in heavy metal and Dungeons & Dragons were far from benign. Social conservatives, as well, saw in the children's accusations extreme proof of the lax permissiveness of liberals, who'd eschewed traditional morality and now were reaping what they'd sown. Most curiously, however, were feminist groups, who found themselves on opposing sides of the debate. Many feminists saw the whole panic as an attack on working mothers, while others saw it as proof both of the dangers of pornography, and the pathological result of a patriarchal culture that failed to take seriously the voices of abused women and children. (When the McMartin preschool was finally razed to the ground, it was Gloria Steinem who paid for the excavation in search of hidden tunnels beneath the building.)

But in the case of the Satanic ritual abuse trials, these groups would in turn be aided by the nascent field of recovered memory hypnosis. The new field was popularized by the book *Michelle Remembers*, written by Lawrence Pazder, a psychiatrist who'd used hypnosis on his patient Michelle Smith to recover a series of memories about a group of Satanists who abused her when she was five. In a trance, she recalled scenes such as one where Satanists dismembered and then reassembled a corpse, reanimating it with electric shocks ("God help me! He cut off its feet! Oh no, I don't want to hear. I can hear him cutting its legs. I can *hear* him cutting the bones up. [...] Oh, God, that's what they're going to do to me next.") Many of Smith's recovered memories contradicted known and incontrovertible facts, and nothing from the book could be corroborated. But the popular reception of books like *Michelle Remembers* and Flora Rheta Schreiber's *Sybil* gave practitioners of recovered memory therapy a foothold and a means of establishing themselves with in the larger psychiatric community.

Little wonder the talk shows ate it up. Oprah Winfrey, Geraldo Rivera, Sally Jessy Raphael, Phil Donahue — the final piece of the puzzle, all of them running breathless testimonials of abuse, terror, ritual, and blood sacrifice. In 1989, long after *Michelle Remembers* had been thoroughly debunked, Oprah invited Smith (who'd since married her psychiatrist Pazder) on as a guest, along with another supposed abuse survivor (Laurel Rose Willson, who'd later reinvent herself as an ersatz Holocaust survivor). Winfrey gave both hoaxers an uncritical platform to spin their wild, unsubstantiated tales to a rapt audience.

In the daytime talk show, the host offers witness and affirmation, while the guest offers her or himself up, blood and body, for immediate consumption by the studio audience and millions of viewers. It is a format designed to generate a kind of pathos, a response to the human soul *in extremis*. Particularly for their primary demographic, stay-at-home mothers, they became a means to escape, if only for a few hours, from the drudgery of the suburbs, a kind of emotional adventurism, a journey through someone else's psyche. The talk shows were perfect peddlers of conspiracies, panics, hoaxes, because truth is of secondary importance to emotional impact. It is no surprise that years after Michelle Smith's appearance, Oprah played host to another hoax memoirist, James Frey, or that she offered a dangerous platform to anti-vaxxer Jenny McCarthy.

Like repressed memory therapy, the talk show is about recovering a testimony, bringing what was hidden into the light. Neither the talk show guest nor the therapy patient is expected to substantiate her or his story with facts or evidence; it is the act of testimony itself which is sufficient, which substantiates itself. If the repressed therapy session was like the confessional booth, the talk show was the tent revival.

Conservative Christians and talk show hosts, psychotherapists and social workers, feminists and anti-feminists: the heart of the Venn diagram where they all overlapped was a fear of the occult. Anti-Christian, defined by an orgiastic quality that could imperil women and children, and a direct rebuke to the notion of a nuclear family — all governed by a fear of ritual abandonment and a loss of self-control.

ꟹ

The fear of secret rituals speaks to something that is, for many people, deeply primal and terrifying. Rituals — particularly those foreign, unknown, or unexplained — strike at the very core of how a society constructs itself. In the cult ritual, bodies writhing in ecstasy, speaking in tongues, engaging in sexual licentiousness, using blood and other bodily fluids — the perfect convergence of threats. An elevated emotional ecstasy offers a kind of dissolution of the self: your boundaries break down, you lose yourself, you become frenzied, bestial, *something not quite human*. In such a state, the normal rules that govern a culture are suspended: laws don't apply, shame and guilt no longer limit activities. Familial and communal bonds — the things that normally govern our behavior, the very heart of the suburban world — cease to have an effect. And traditional authority figures — the priest, the police officer, the governmental authority, the head of the household — are replaced with hierarchical figures of unknown provenance. If we fear the specter of such rituals, it's because they offer the chance to dissolve all of the normal restraints that govern middle-class life and replace them with an entirely different set of values that cannot be restrained or controlled in the usual manner.

The Reagan '80s were in every way about selfishness, about asserting oneself and one's own needs over others. Cults offered a most radical rebuke to this individualism: an inverted world where there is no self, where you are not yourself, not in charge of yourself — and afterward, you are not even in control of your own memories, which bear no trace of how much of yourself you've lost. It was the perfect hysteria for the inherently uncanny feeling of living in suburbs, feeding the fear of what other people were doing in their own homes. Alone at home with the TV on in the background, dwellers of the suburbs peered through the blinds and wondered if the neighbors were letting themselves go.

Vivan Sundaram, Detail of *Stone Column Enclosing the Gaze*, from the series Collaboration/Combines, 1992.
Sandstone, acrylic sheet, b&w photographs, mirror and enamel. 213.36 x 45.72 x 45.72 cm.
Image courtesy of the artist.

THE MEAL

ELISABETH HOUSTON

There she was, a pink
wrinkled thing, spat out

on a fine china plate.
Who would have thought

a baby could be born
from a mouth, from two

dark, wormy lips? Nearby,
the fork and knife lie on a napkin

and contemplate their dead marriage.
Mother takes the fork

and Father pours some wine,
while Chopin rises like steam

from the record.

THE HOUSE IN THE HAGUE

KATHRYN DAVIS

It began as a joke. My wife was dying. She only had so much time left — how much, we didn't know. Her spirits were generally good, meaning we spent our mornings sitting side by side in bed, drinking coffee and reading the local paper, all 10 pages of it. The dog was at our feet, the kitten sucking on the comforter. Personal details about your private life are made public today, my wife said, reading my horoscope. Meanwhile, you need more sleep. Well, duh. The room has four large windows, facing east, the direction of the rising sun, the waxing moon, Rabbit, Air, Redemption. The way the house is situated, on a small rise overlooking Carondelet Street, what you see out the bedroom windows are the branches of locust trees framing pieces of winter sky shaped like puzzle pieces, the kind of puzzles I had as a boy where some pieces were shaped like things, a horn, a bicycle wheel, a shoe. My favorite was a scene showing birds standing one-legged in a marsh at sunset, the sun pouring all sorts of colors across the water. It made no sense for a high-heeled shoe to be there. This is what I think about while my dying wife reads to me from the local paper.

And the wind. And the drops of rain like bullets. Gros Morne, the final pitch a sheer wall of scree, and there it was, lying on the wet talus, a red high-heeled shoe.

It was at about this time an old college girlfriend and her husband put down a deposit on a house in The Hague, and when I showed my wife the pictures she said it made her sad that after all the money and work we'd put into our house — and she enumerated, bookshelves, stonewalls, bookshelves, walls, shelves, shelves! (for over the years we both came to own many books we were loath to part with) — after all that, my wife said, not to mention the blue spruce out front, a baby when we planted it and just think of it now, how could she dream of leaving? She stared at me intently, her eyes ever so slightly crossing in that endearing way of hers.

Ruth says the city's infrastructure is in worse shape than I am, my wife said, and it was simple enough to conflate her friend's view of our sewer system with the occult data on the disks we're handed by the good-natured woman whose job it is to keep track of the story unfolding in my wife's internal organs. A few snowflakes fell through the puzzle pieces. Only a few — the big ones that augur nothing.

I'd entertained the possibility that I might look up that old girlfriend, later. After.
bai and bai.

But you don't have to leave the house, I said. You could haunt it.

What was I thinking? I wasn't thinking anything. Though just before: The road bent left. The blood flow was unceasing. I dreamed I was picking red flowers. To the right a large tree of some kind beginning to leaf out, one gray asbestos-tile wall of the general store visible behind it. By summer the green Valvoline advertisement no longer in view. The eyes staring fixedly without blinking. The scaling of the mountain of the elements. Place the wrist at the point between the eyebrows. The arm so thin as to be a line and then it's gone!

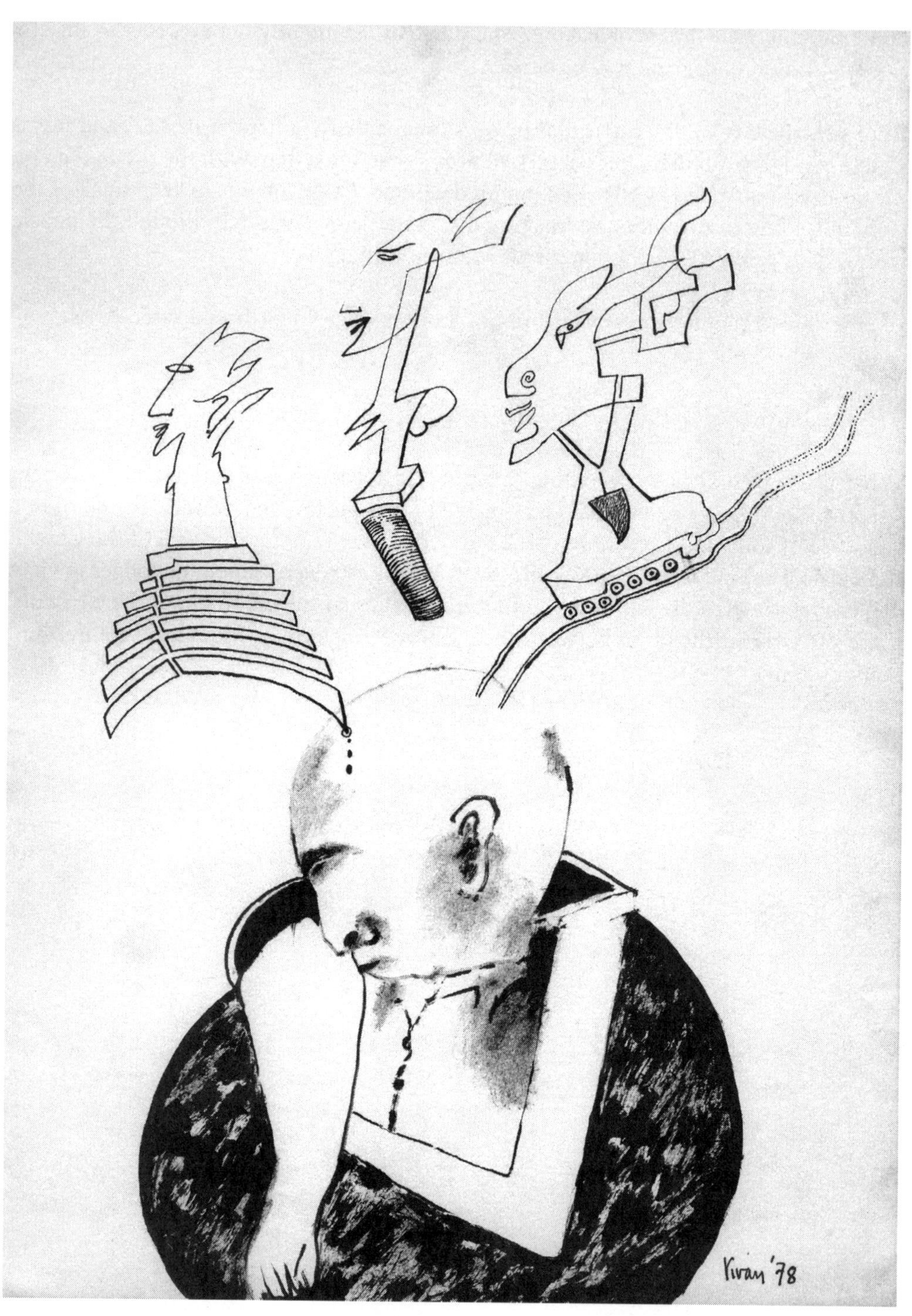

Vivan Sundaram, *Untitled*, from the series Drawings Mexico. Material ink on paper. 27.94 x 35.56 cm.
Image courtesy of the artist.

THE DESPERATE SEARCH FOR THE MARK OF THE BEAST

ANNA MERLAN

"I have a lot of anxiety and fear about not being saved," a woman who identified herself as a Baptist wrote in the summer of 2017, on a message board called Christian Forums. "[B]ut don't know how to be saved. I have been afraid of the unpardonable sin (Matthew 12, Mark 3, Luke 12), the mark of the beast [...] even the number six by itself sets off impulsive thoughts."

Earlier this year, in Reddit's r/Christianity forum, another user shared a similar anxiety, edged with terror. "I was just wondering if anyone else has these feelings about the mark," she wrote. "Sometimes I panic and wonder if I'm already marked or if smartphones are the mark. I was wondering other's thoughts about it. My husband is not a Christian so he usually tells me to stop worrying about it."

These are contemporary forums for expressing an almost ancient fear. Worried Christians have long agonized over salvation, experiencing a feeling that has been recently dubbed, with a nod to our therapy-obsessed age, "salvation anxiety." A significant part of that anxiety — as well as the exact place where American Christianity merges with right-wing conspiracy theory — is the Mark of the Beast.

The Mark is mentioned in the Book of Revelation, the New Testament's beautiful, baffling, and terrifying final book. Revelation, believed to have been written by John the Apostle, reads like a series of unanswered riddles. Some historians and theologists take it to be an allegory about life under the Roman Empire, while some Christian theorists read it as set of predictions, yet to unfold. For those Christians who follow a philosophy broadly known as futurism, the book is specifically a set of prophecies: the Rapture, the Great Tribulation — a period of terrible suffering for those left on earth — the reign of the Antichrist, the Second Coming, the resurrection of the dead, and the Final Judgment. Exactly when the events will occur, and in what order, is a subject of heated debate and more than a little sectarian squabbling. If the reign of the Antichrist is still in the future, that would mean that the Mark and Number of the Beast, too, are yet to be unleashed on the world.

It's unclear who or what the Beast is, precisely; Revelation talks about two monstrous beings, one that emerges from the sea, and another, somewhat later, from the earth. They seem to be a kind of advance team for the Antichrist. The Mark of the Beast is the first sign of the coming terrors and the realization of the Antichrist's sovereignty over the earth.

Spotting the first signs of the Antichrist's appearance has long been a subject of fascination and speculation among many Christian groups. As the message boards make clear, the anxiety over seeing these signs is still strong, particularly among American evangelicals. Mitch Horowitz, the author of *Occult America* and an expert on esoteric religious thought in American life, pointed out in a recent interview that these fears show the outsize influence Revelation has had on American culture and popular religious thought. Revelation, he says, "has served as this kind of backwards filter for people on the rest of Scripture. Passages that were otherwise intended to refer to local conflicts or a dispute with a local ruler or the duality of God became reinterpreted as the personification of an adversary, of evil." Had Revelation not been canonized — had it remained apocryphal as many other religious texts written around the same time — Horowitz says, "Our whole religious culture would be different. Concepts like the Mark of the Beast or the Apocalypse or even the personification of Satan would be on the fringes of society, instead of the voluminous place they occupy in popular culture."

Instead, prophecies and predictions of the End Times have become mainstream. Many believe that the series of events leading up to Armageddon and the Second Coming can be decoded by close-reading the Bible, particularly Revelation and the Book of Daniel. To that end, the several lines in Revelation regarding the Mark have been the subject of fervent study:

> And he causes all, the small and the great, and the rich and the poor, and the free men and the slaves, to be given a mark on their right hand or on their forehead, and he provides that no one will be able to buy or to sell, except the one who has the mark, either the name of the beast or the number of his name. Here is wisdom. Let him who has understanding calculate the number

> of the beast, for the number is that of a man; and his number is six hundred and sixty-six.

These lines, because of their interpretative obscurity, can be read in thousands of ways. Often, readings are applied to current events or contemporary figures (some for example, believe that Trump is a sign of the second coming). Either way, these words have become a subject of urgent, fevered speculation, a mixture of both hope and terrible fear.

ജ്ഞ

Twentieth-century Christian futurists have seen the Mark many times over. Some of the uptick in End Times theorizing can be traced back to the early 1970s and the influence of one man, Hal Lindsey. Lindsey, an evangelical writer and television host, published a blockbuster book called *The Late, Great Planet Earth*, which prophesied that the Antichrist would come in the 1970s and the Rapture would come in the 1980s. Lindsey wrote many follow-ups, including *Satan Is Alive and Well on Planet Earth* and *The 1980's: Countdown to Armageddon*. Lindsey's writing had an enormous effect on popular evangelical thought, making the previously dry subject of Christian eschatology and Biblical close-reading into something both accessible and tantalizing: a doctrinally acceptable way of foretelling the future. (Some theologians sniffed that Lindsey's thinking wasn't particularly fresh, but instead a simplified version of the work of John Nelson Darby, an Irish Anglican priest who died in 1882 and who's considered to be the father of Christian futurism. Darby taught that Christians would be secretly raptured from the Earth in advance of the Great Tribulation.) Tim LaHaye and Jerry B. Jenkins's *Left Behind* series, whose first volume appeared in 1995, has followed in Lindsey's footsteps. Both series were astonishingly successful, and helped create a tidy, ever-expanding End Times cottage industry. Both series also encouraged a keener eye for the Mark of the Beast.

Barcodes were one of the earliest objects of this modern form of salvation anxiety. They were introduced in 1973 — directly beneath the long shadow of Lindsey's *The Late, Great Planet Earth* — and were immediately the subject of dire warnings from evangelical Christians. Barcodes were also part of many surprisingly durable urban legends (for instance, the story that every barcode contains the number 666, which Snopes has gone out of its way to debunk).

The entire concept of a cashless society has provoked similar foreboding. This fear can partly be traced back to another emerging technology: RFID chips. While radio frequency identification technology has been around since World War II, RFID tags became much more common in the early 2000s, used in credit cards, cars, and as microchips embedded underneath the skin of livestock. This proliferation caught the attention of many apocalypse-facing Christian groups, but the embedded chip raised the most alarm. The alarm only grew louder when tech publications like *Wired* started reporting, around 2003, that companies would soon start offering microchips that could be embedded under the skin of humans and used as a form of payment.

More recently, another a new technology emerging as a potential Mark: cryptocurrency, which the End Times author Britt Gillette has proclaimed to be the closest thing yet to the economic system Revelations describes. "In order to control who can buy and who can sell, the Antichrist will need a system capable of tracking every transaction on earth," he wrote in 2018. "Cryptocurrencies and public block chain records provide such a system."

The search for the mark goes beyond technology however. As the Antichrist stubbornly refuses to make his appearance — most mainstream evangelical thinkers believe the Antichrist is indeed a "he," and likely to come from the European Union — the theorizing and the fears have become more closely aligned with secular right-wing fears about government overreach, manipulation, and insidious methods of control.

The particular place where secular far-right groups and Christian extremists overlap is the idea of the so-called "New World Order," a term that right-wing extremists and militia movements use to mean a system of tyrannical one-world government enslaving us all. Beginning in the 1970s — and reaching a fever pitch in the 1990s, after George H. W. Bush used the term "New World Order" in a speech — secular far-right groups and some Christian futurists alike started to warn that the United Nations or some other global body were planning an impending takeover of the United States.

In some cases, Christianity and the far-right overlapped, producing a genus of Christian extremists like The Covenant, The Sword, and The Arm of the Lord (CSA), a group that grew out of a Baptist congregation in the 1970s, and whose leader, minister James Ellison, preached that a race war was impending and "God's people," white Christians, needed "an Ark." The CSA eventually created a heavily fortified Arkansas compound, which dissolved under a massive federal raid in 1985; the group was found to be stockpiling potassium cyanide as part of a plan to poison the water supply and hasten the Second Coming. Though the CSA raid ended when its leaders surrendered peacefully, the federal government subsequently used a much more heavy-handed response during two other standoffs with groups with strong religious ties: the Weaver family at Ruby Ridge, Idaho, in 1992 and the Branch Davidian compound in Waco, Texas, in 1993. The Weaver matriarch Vicki, her son Sammy and their dog Striker were killed by federal agents. After several days of the standoff at Waco, federal agents began spraying tear gas into the compound and the government says the Branch Davidians began then setting fires throughout the compound. Some survivors of the attack have accused the government of setting the fires. In all, 76 people died in the fires, including 25 children.

Though they were the most dramatic, these violent events weren't the last time that secular right-wing and Christian conspiracy theories would coincide. In his 1999 book

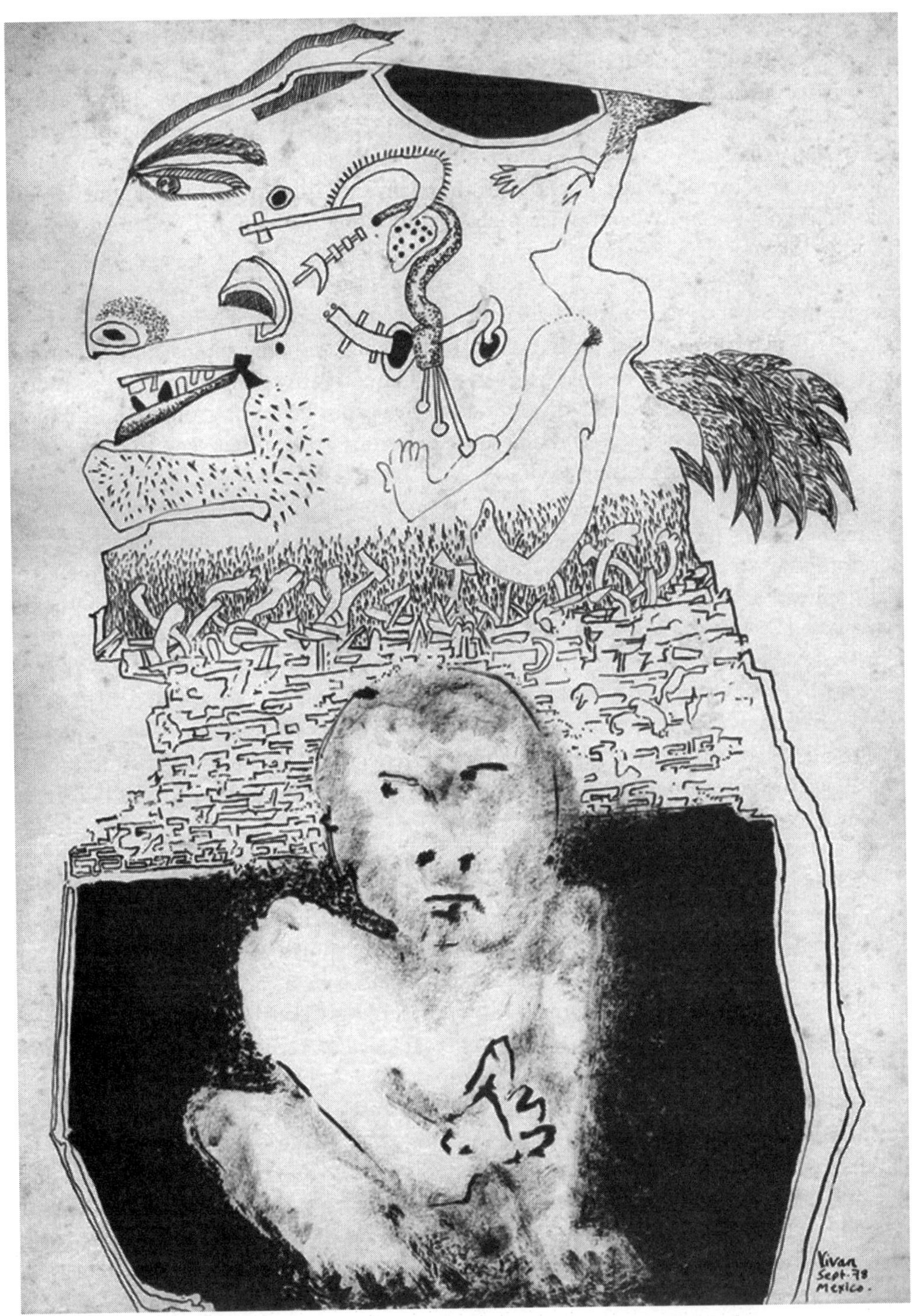

Vivan Sundaram, *Untitled*, from the series Drawings Mexico, 1978. Ink on paper. 27.94 cm x 35.56 cm.
Image courtesy of the artist

Conspiracy Theories: Secrecy and Power in American Culture, the author and professor Mark Fenster points out that Christian conspiracy theories, particularly those around the Apocalypse, tend to mirror secular right-wing conspiracy theories, in ways that strengthen and reinforce both sides. "Many popular eschatological texts lean towards right-wing conspiracy theory," he wrote, "Particularly in their patriotism, fears of a one-world government, virulent anti-Communism and calls for a strong military — all of which would seem to contradict their sublime longing for Christ's return from a spiritual realm of which humans have no power."

Fenster notes that conservative Christianity has a "tendency to view historical and current events in terms of vast conspiracies led by knowing and unwitting agents of Satan." Seen that way, he writes, it's not surprising that conservative Christians find so much common ground with the John Birch Society and other far right groups, all of which see the world "as the domain of secret and dangerous groups that seek to undermine and destroy Christian beliefs and values."

Evangelical fears about the Satanic undermining of society have faced plenty of scoffing from mainstream, secular types. But fears about broad surveillance, about the ethical implications of a cashless society, about the constant tradeoffs we make between privacy and security, aren't wild-eyed conspiracy theorizing, they aren't limited to the Christian right, and they aren't hard to understand. (Nor are they new: In *The Handmaid's Tale*, for instance, a key plot point is that women are deprived access to their bank accounts overnight because the system has been so centralized.) Conspiratorial ideas tend to be a particularly fervid and intense reflection of mainstream culture, and a fear about the government tracking and microchipping us for insidious ends becomes, frankly, less outlandish with every passing year.

There's also no denying that some aspects of centralized government control are more of a concern for those on the right. Irvin Baxter is a genial, politically conservative Pentecostal televangelist based in Texas whose entire ministry — fittingly called End Times Ministries — is oriented toward what he and others call the "end of the age." Over the years, he has issued warnings himself about RFID chips and cashless technologies; more recently, he's also speculated that the REAL ID Act and Obamacare are precursors to the Mark, because both programs sought to impose greater federal regulation on state-run systems, namely drivers' licenses and the health insurance markets. Baxter, like Lindsey, has written about the dangers of a cashless society in ways designed to appeal to both the Apocalypse-fearing and IRS-loathing parts of his audience. "In a cashless society, no one will be in jail for bank robbery because there will be nothing to steal," he wrote in an undated post about the Mark of the Beast. "Also, a cashless society is very attractive to the IRS, because, if the government has records of everything you do, it will be able to withdraw taxes from your income before you have a chance to spend it."

Despite the popularity of figures like Baxter, End Times prophecies and the hunt for the Mark of the Beast remain fringe (Randall Palmer, chair of the religious studies department at Dartmouth College, who's also an Episcopal priest, speaking to the *Tennessean* in 2017, politely called them a "parlor game"). Among those who believe, though there are a riot of competing theories, one commonality remains: many End Times theorists are convinced that whatever the Mark is, it's already here. "Our mistake is to assume that The Mark of the Beast is an artifact of the future," says the surprisingly conspiratorial Catholic Online, one of the largest internet resources for Catholics. "It has already arrived. Therefore, since it is a sign, we would do well to prepare ourselves for the final hour could come at any time."

Vivan Sundaram, Detail of *Stone Column Enclosing the Gaze*, from the series Collaboration/Combines, 1992.
Sandstone, acrylic sheet, b&w photographs, mirror, and enamel. 213.36 x 45.72 x 45.72 cm.
Image courtesy of the artist.

CONCERNING THE MEANING MOLECULE IN POETRY

BRENDA HILLMAN

Long ago a man told me, If you write poetry
keep your subjects small;

i was a tiny skinny girl at that point …

Much later, i heard a meaning molecule
in the call of a dove pretending to be an owl in the pine,

a song-speck circling in a thought throughout all time
(like the man said, *extremely* small!)

traveling from before literature
through the blue centuries until quite recently

when a radiant instance of the unknown

paused our bafflement but kept
that little meaning absolutely elusive, & erotic …

for AC & NS

Vivan Sundaram, *Allegorical landscape II*, 1987-1988. Charcoal on paper. 30 x 40 cm.
Image courtesy of the artist.

THE SLEEPING ILLNESS

MASANDE NTSHANGA

There were times my father's drinking could get the better of him. Pa would walk in from a tavern with scars hatched across his forearms like a trawling net, and I couldn't keep his clothes on him when it was time to set him down for sleep.

It would happen mostly during winter.

The nighttime twisted his thinking.

He'd kick at the walls of our box and swear, raising our pots, and then he'd begin to strip himself bare. I'd have to stoke a fire for the paraffin stove before heaving it inside. The rain would tap over the lid and the hearth and I would watch as the flames tinted the mesh dome a bright orange — a color that often put him to sleep.

I was thinking about him, again, that morning, when I heard about The Golden Fowl.

How he'd walked back into town to claim his flock.

I hadn't slept the previous night, sick from treating a man who'd put his hands on a child. He didn't deserve his next breath. He was back on his feet now, but had left me with nausea — an ache in each joint, wrong-headedness. The previous night, when I'd touched him on his kitchen floor, summoning him back through my amulet and loam, he'd shot through me like a geyser, painting my insides black with his sickness. Inathi said we could find an herb for me in District Six.

"The Holes?"

He nodded. I was seated with him at a cafe at the train station, hunched over a corner table. I watched the buses pass behind him as he ate. He kept his eyes on the paper plate. Our clothes smelled of smoke.

"It's between Rutger and Reform," he said, pulling a Vienna sausage off a bed of chips. I'd offered to feed it to him. He tore the pink meat in two. "Do you know them?"

Most of us who worked in remedies did. I knew how the men there used the sewer flow to rinse their bodies and how they knocked on their neighbors' doors for cooking water.

"He's reliable," Inathi said, looking up from his plate. "He won't charge much."

The sun brightened behind him. Its light fell in a yellow haze over the smog, and commuters blurred into it as they walked past the door, silhouetted like reeds bent forward in a breeze. A handful of them streamed into the cafe, raising the chatter, and I leaned back to watch them queue up to eat.

Our lines often reminded me of a feeding trough. Those who reached the front pawed at the glass that held the meat inside trapped air: trays of tripe, liver, and sheep's head, and they sated themselves with their eyes before they ate.

That's what The Golden Fowl used to tell us in 2008.

He often compared us to beasts of the wild. He admonished the abundance of oil at our stores, and told us to keep away from the excesses of salt. Most of us were too tired to heed him at first. We thought he looked the way he did from a fortune stuck in the womb.

༺༻

Inathi was almost done. I pushed a cup of water toward him.

"I'll give you the package when we come back," I said.

He sucked on his teeth. "That's a trip going both ways for me."

"You won't pay."

"No?"

"No."

"Good."

༺༻

We took the lane up Station Road before we turned into Main. We crossed over two more lanes and waited for an ice truck on the third. I wanted to be free of him, I thought. I didn't think he was suited for the job. I asked him about his aunt — the woman who'd raised him.

"I heard she died in a fire," he said.

"Where?"

"The one in '05."

I remembered. The columns of smoke had risen from the west. The boxes in Joe Slovo had caught alight from an open flame used to heat a pot of diced cabbage, and it had carried in the wind, leaping from one box to the other. Later, the smoke had darkened the horizon on the west coast for a day, and the next morning, 10,000 boxes had been reduced to rubble. The residents were now migrated to Delft, at a greater distance from work, and kept frozen on the city's housing lists. The boxes that held them now had walls that came apart, with sand rising up through their linoleum and blowing into their sheets, their sacks of maize meal.

I told Inathi I'd pay for us on the way back, and he was quiet as we walked across the next lane. "We're almost there," he said, and we were.

We crossed Sir Lowry Road and started up the hill toward District Six. The clouds parted over us as we walked, and I could feel the sun tether itself to my forehead, drawing out beads of sweat. I thought of Pa again.

There were times when he could pull himself away from the bottle, during our first years at the boxes, before he got struck by what he called "a burden on his side." He used to rinse his Lion razors and shear his beard, but it never lasted for more than a week. He'd arrive at our box with his fists clenched and his one foot wavering behind the other. I could tell whenever he'd been drinking. He said he needed the fog in his head to deal with his work. How his work made him sick.

"I usually take laxatives," I told Inathi.

"Laxatives?"

"They get the job done. I can't do anything until I'm cleared."

He bent down to light a cigarette. I often told him about the job to ward him off it, but he never reacted. "Raising a man packs the colon with poison," I said.

Inathi shrugged. "My aunt used to say it was dangerous to loosen yourself like that, with pills."

I thought of The Golden Fowl, again, and how he'd often found similar poisons in our habits. His name could still stun us into silence and wonder. Here was a man who could make a son dance at his mother's funeral, we said.

ꕤ

The holes dug into the field were visible — even from our distance — and each one had a man standing guard over its mouth. These were the caves we'd come to know the district for. The Holes. Their entrances were misshapen, as if a large hand had reached down and dug its fingers through the soil. Inathi and I found torn plastic sheets strewn across the field, and on top of them a collection of blankets, buckets, and charred pots without handles.

"I heard they've dug out more holes since that shooting in Delft," he said.

It was true, but I didn't answer. I let him go on.

"I've heard the work's started to dry up in the city," he said. "Everyone wants to get on the back of a bakkie and the bosses know it."

He was right about the growth in residents. Earlier that year, there'd been evictions in Delft, and close to a thousand residents had been poured out onto Symphony Road, towing their belongings behind them in the heat. They'd vowed to sleep on the road, that night, until they could be returned to their homes, and most of them had begun to, when the police had woken them up with live rounds.

We walked into the field, and Inathi pointed us to a man sitting on a large rock. He was squinting, pinching the filter on his cigarette, and his shoulder muscles churned as he released the smoke through his nostrils. He took a while to turn when we got to him. Then he put the cigarette out on the rock and laughed at Inathi's question.

"No, we don't have herbs here," he smiled.

Vivan Sundaram, *Archaeology of War III,* 1987-1988. Charcoal on paper, 70 x 100 cm.
Image courtesy of the artist

"Take us to Ta Maanda, then," Inathi said. "He's got herbs on him."

"He's gone," the man shrugged. "We didn't get to keep his things." He turned and looked behind him. "You can see there's nothing left, here."

I looked. Everything they owned sat outside the caves.

"You're all moving?"

"You haven't heard?"

"Heard what?"

His eyes narrowed. "Where did you come from?"

"Mowbray."

"You must've heard then."

Inathi and I were silent. The man smiled.

"The Golden Fowl," he said. "He was seen him coming out of the ocean in Milnerton. There was a boy who ran here to tell us his clothes where dry."

We still didn't answer.

I looked behind me and saw another man in blue overalls approaching us from the field. He nodded at the two of us before turning to the man.

"I think that's everything."

"Everyone's been looked at?"

The other man nodded. "We've pulled them all out."

"Good. He can never see us like this."

He got off the rock and nodded at us. Then the two of them walked back to The Holes. Inathi and I made our way to the edge of the field before we heard the first crackle and turned, which is when we saw them light the first fires inside the holes.

"It's true, then," Inathi said. "He's back."

I asked him what he'd heard.

"Not much."

"Not much?"

"There's a laaitie in town who says he's the devil."

CARDIOLOGIST

WILLIAM BREWER

Her eyebrows twitching
just as I knew they would, just as I knew
the desk plant would bow under central air,
rain whipping the window, each
moment like looking at a photograph
of what's already happened happening
soft with afterglow
as she explains how the whoosh
coming over the sonogram
is blood leaking through my valve,
which I knew already. I've heard it
almost all my life, back to a Halloween
when I was found collapsed in a yard,
a black bat sprawled on fallen maple,
the sky draining its harvest blue,
the same blue of the latex gloves
I knew the cardiologist would put on,
then did, just before she slid
the jellied doppler-node over my chest
like the planchette on a Ouija board,
favorite pastime of my babysitter.
I'd study the soft touch of her hands
and wait for her to abandon it; then,
once alone, try to call myself in the beyond,
but what I said I can't remember.

BREADWINNER

WILLIAM BREWER

I am not hiding from the night—
more like preparing for it. Waiting for its signals.
Above me the bedsprings sewn up in stained canvas on the old frame.
My breathing slowed
to slow my mind.
I go very still, press my mouth to the floor
and try to keep my exhales from moving the dust
to where the surgical light of the streetlamp
glazes the rug.
Right on time:
the driveway crackling awake, the hole punched in the air
when the engine goes dead.
Because I cannot stand the sound
of how the day has changed his walk—
worn boot soles buffing
the lime-washed pine of the porch,
does his limp drag, does he kick
the baseboard, a code relaying
whether we will eat from the white plates
waiting on the handmade table,
or if one will fly across the room and turn to dust against the wall—
I press my hands to my ears and listen
to the oceanic rush of blood in my temples,
try to imagine a sea past the sea that keeps going out,
green into green, the spinning stones cracked smaller.
And then the squish
of his steps through the garden
to the shed where he sits alone,
assembling and taking apart, over and over, the same machine.

CANNIBAL

ANNA JOURNEY

I've been thinking a lot about cannibals lately. Fairy tale cannibals. Biblio-cannibals. I've been thinking about books eating books. Several months ago, I received an email from a stranger named Jodi, who wrote to notify me of my act of accidental cannibalism. Jodi told me that I'd stolen her young daughter's innocence, that I needed to do something to stop other children from losing their innocence, too.

The situation involved a literary switcheroo: a bizarre accident at a book bindery. My writing, I learned, had inadvertently cannibalized a *New York Times* best-selling children's novel. Two essays from my nonfiction collection appear as chapters in Jodi's daughter's edition of *The Girl Who Drank the Moon*, by fantasy author Kelly Barnhill. At some point during the binding process, my book's third signature — a unit of bound pages — replaced the third signature of the children's novel. Barnhill's *The Girl Who Drank the Moon* features a spunky little witch-girl named Luna who lives in the woods with her adopted family: Fyrian, an ecstatic, Chihuahua-sized dragon; Glerk, a serene, poetry-quoting swamp monster; and Xan, a loving yet grumbly old witch. Xan had rescued baby Luna from a barbaric ritual in which a group of village elders had left the infant in the forest to die. In trying to revive the baby, Xan mistakenly gave Luna a drink of potent moonlight instead of mellow starlight. The child then developed supernatural powers that grew increasingly turbulent as Luna approached her teens.

The Girl Who Drank the Moon — aimed at children 10 to 14 — is advertised as "an epic coming-of-age fairy tale." Throughout Barnhill's nearly 400-page book, Luna's adolescence looms as an allegorized threat that recalls many familiar tropes about "uncontrollable" women: moons and madness, lunacy and menstruation. "It was starting early," Barnhill writes of the girl's intensifying magic. "All that power — the great surging ocean of it — was leaking out." The well-meaning Xan casts a spell to stunt Luna's magic, temporarily cocooning the girl, like a moth or Sleeping Beauty, so the young witch won't set the forest on fire or turn her loved ones into rabbits. Xan needs more time to teach Luna how to wield her lunar gifts. At the end of the novel, Luna emerges from her stasis to save the people of the neighboring village, the Protectorate, from a fascist council of elders and an evil nemesis-witch.

My essays — "The Guineveres" and "Strange Merchants" — consume pages 55–87 of Jodi's daughter's book. "The Guineveres" explores my mother's penchant for telling macabre tales at the dinner table, while "Strange Merchants" riffs on the theme of "the stranger." In the mutant novel — the Frankenbook — Kelly Barnhill's work stops after the following paragraphs:

> "Come down this instant, young lady," the Witch hollered.
>
> The little girl laughed. She flitted toward the ground, leaping from leaf to leaf, guiding the other children safely behind her. Xan could see the tendrils of magic fluttering behind her like ribbons. Blue and silver, silver and blue. They billowed and swelled and spiraled in the air.

On the next page, my essay "The Guineveres" starts:

> My mother's always marveled at Ted Bundy's charisma, his trick with the fake injuries, his voluminous hairdo. Throughout my childhood she'd recite the serial killer's murderous steps like a mantra — the arm sling, the dropped stack of books, the women Bundy shoved into his white Volkswagen Beetle. "Don't ever get into a stranger's car," she warned my younger sister and me.

In that same paragraph, I recall my mom's other storytelling obsessions: Trotsky, the exiled Marxist who died by an assassin's ice axe; Travis, the pet chimpanzee who gnawed off a woman's face; and Rosie, the 10-year-old girl from our northern Virginia suburb who was kidnapped, smothered, and dumped beneath a pine tree.

After "The Guineveres," my essay "Strange Merchants" proceeds through Barnhill's interrupted tale. In "Strange Merchants," I recount how my father once bought a leather trench coat, at a Bolivian airport, from an older German immigrant who may have been a Nazi in hiding. The timing — late '70s — and the place would've been about right. I also mention my parents' ex-pat term in Germany:

> In 1975 my mother and father moved to Peine, in the German state of Lower Saxony, so my father could begin a research position in a plastic pipe manufacturing plant. For a year they lived just three miles from the memorial grounds of Bergen-Belsen. My mother asked my dad several times to come with her to visit the site of the former concentration camp, but he refused. Although my father remains a formidable history buff who can discuss with encyclopedic precision the finer points of World War II — battles, geographical terrain,

> political figures — the subject of the death camp stirs in him a crushing, unfathomable horror so extreme he can't bring himself to discuss it. (He feels a distinctive yet similarly acute sense of dread about the void of deep space.) Occasionally he deflects his horror of the concentration camps through humor, singing, for instance, the British song mocking the Nazi leadership called "Hitler Has Only Got One Ball," which assumes the campy, jingle-like cadences of the marching tune "Colonel Bogey March."

"I have text-chatted, called and posted and can't get Amazon to stop selling this version of the book," Jodi wrote. "My goal," she continued, "is that no other young girl working on her Battle of the Books reading list loses some of her innocence asking parents about serial killers, Hitler's genitalia, anal rodent penetration, etc etc."

"Anal rodent penetration," I said, squinting at the email. "Huh. Can't place that one." I handed my phone to my husband, David, who began laughing as he read the message. I soon recognized the reference from one of my essays — a high-schooler's silly taunt: "Matt sticks hamsters up his butt." I ordered a copy of *The Girl Who Drank the Moon*, hoping for a corrupted text (no luck), and wrote Jodi back. I was so sorry for the bewildering situation, I told her; I'd notify both publishers at once. Although I spoke with several surprised representatives of each press, no one could explain what had happened, exactly, or tell me how many Frankenbooks the bindery accident might have spawned. Hundreds? Dozens? A single mangled one? Call it *Dark Side of the Moon*, David suggested. Or *The Girl Who Was Mooned*, quipped my best friend, Alicia.

ꟹ

By the time the crescent moon slid past the windowsill and peeked into the room, Fyrian was snoring. By the time the moon shone fully through the window, he had begun to singe Luna's nightgown. And by the time the curve of the moon touched the opposite window frame, Fyrian's breath made a bright red mark on the side of Luna's hip, leaving a blister there.

ꟹ

"Undress and get into bed with me," says the wolf in a folktale told by peasants throughout early modern France. The wolf had met a girl in the woods and tricked her into telling him the route to her grandmother's house. He raced to the cottage, killed the old woman, poured her blood into a bottle, chopped up her flesh, and offered the girl, when she arrived, a cannibal's snack. "Slut!" cried a cat. "To eat the flesh and drink the blood of your grandmother!"

This gory tale later morphed into Charles Perrault's "Little Red Riding Hood." Cultural historian Robert Darnton, in his book *The Great Cat Massacre*, traces the evolution of the story from its origins in popular oral tradition to its absorption into the fashionable literary genre of fairy tale. Perrault's readers, Darnton notes, were the bourgeois salon sophisticates of the late 1600s — not the illiterate peasantry — so the French author cut the troubling cannibalism and added a scene in which the girl dis-

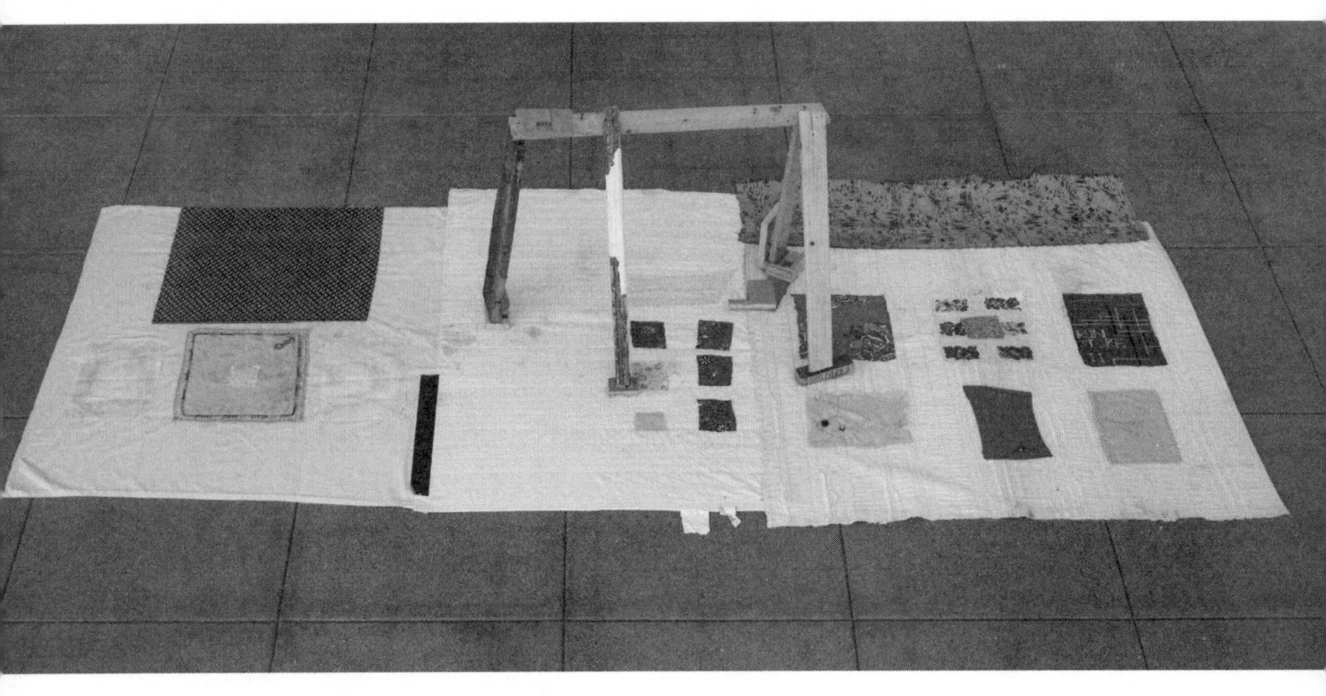

Susan Cianciolo, *Patchwork Geometry 4*, 2018. Textiles, paper, pastel, glue, nails, and wood. 6 x 140 x 72 1/2 inches. Image courtesy of the Overduin & Co., Los Angeles

obeys her mother's advice (to justify the child's demise) as well as a moral about the importance of not falling prey to smooth-talking strangers. Perrault also added that iconic red cap. During the 19th century, German authors Jacob and Wilhelm Grimm grafted onto Perrault's French fairy tale a happy ending in which a hunter hears thunderous snores as he passes the house, discovers the wolf dozing in bed, and slits the beast's belly with shears, freeing Little Red Riding Hood and her grandmother. The girl fills the wolf's stomach with rocks, so that when he wakes up and tries to flee, he's felled by his own stony weight. "Little Red Riding Hood went cheerfully home," the Brothers Grimm write, "and came to no harm."

The French peasants told their folktales about the girl and the wolf from the 15th to the 18th century, during fireside gatherings in which women sewed and men sharpened tools. Many peasant versions of "Little Red Riding Hood" are amoral and barbaric, terrifyingly irrational. In addition to cannibalism, one rendition of the story evokes bestiality, murder, and a flamboyant striptease. "Where shall I put my apron?" the girl asks the wolf:

> "Throw it on the fire; you won't need it anymore."
>
> For each garment — bodice, skirt, petticoat, and stockings — the girl asked the same question; and each time the wolf answered, "Throw it on the fire; you won't need it anymore."

The story ends with a single sentence: "And he ate her." There's no wayward girl, as in Perrault's character, no Grimm Brothers' hunter *ex machina*. Yet not all of the versions of the peasant tale are unhappy. In some of them, the girl survives, but not because of her goodness or piety: she's a canny trickster who fools the wolf by saying she has to go outside to pee: "I have to relieve myself, Grandmother."

❧

"I have to go to the bathroom," I told my therapist when I was 15, glancing at the cop she'd called, presumably to escort me, if necessary, to the adolescent wing of Dominion Hospital. She'd explained the inpatient psychiatric treatment plan as the officer lingered in the doorway. I wore black patent boots, a leather biker bodice, and the bottom half of my little sister's cut-off ballet tutu. My hair color: Manic Panic's "Flamingo Pink." I'd been burning my arms with cigarettes and a steel coat hanger heated with a lighter. Halfway down the hall to the restroom, I looked back. Neither my shrink nor the cop had followed me. I rode the elevator to the ground floor, scrambled across the parking lot and through the woods that horseshoed the strip mall, and dodged two lanes of afternoon traffic to reach the chain restaurant Bob Evans. "My dentist appointment got canceled," I told the hostess. "May I call my mom from your phone?" Afterward, I crouched between cars in the restaurant's parking lot, waiting for my friend's white van to pull up as I sweated in the early spring heat.

❧

The day was warm and sticky, and she realized with creeping horror that she was starting to stink. This sort of thing had been happening a lot lately — bad smells, strange eruptions on her face. Luna felt as though every single thing on her body had suddenly conspired to alter itself — even her voice had turned traitorous.

ꟸ

Psychoanalyst Erich Fromm interprets "Little Red Riding Hood" as a coming-of-age fairy tale in which a pubescent girl confronts the onset of adolescence. To Fromm, the red hood symbolizes menstruation; the bottle she carries represents her virginity; the mother's warning not to stray into wild terrain alludes to sexual promiscuity; and the stones the girl places in the wolf's belly imply her punishment for climbing into bed with a stranger: sterility. The problem is, Darnton notes, Fromm's symbols don't exist in the peasant folktales. Fromm reads the story as if it's free-floating, completely ahistorical, universal in its tropes. If fairy tales strike us as timeless, it's because so many people have revised them in the telling, shuffling centuries of customs and beliefs. Child psychologist Bruno Bettelheim sees in "Little Red Riding Hood" an opportunity for children to reckon with repressed Oedipal desires, though there's nothing particularly repressed or subtle about the earlier tale's fiery, bodice-flinging striptease. Kids can work through their fears, Bettelheim suggests, within the safety of the tale's affirmative ending, assuming, of course, that the ending is indeed a happy one. Both Fromm and Bettelheim believe in a single fixed narrative when in fact there are many. They invent a falsely stable text that was never cannibalized with red caps and helpful hunters or revised for the bourgeoisie. They imagine only one girl makes her way through the woods when there's a multiplicity.

ꟸ

"I know my daughter wasn't your intended audience," Jodi wrote. "Please have your attorneys contact Amazon. Please save another young family from going through this."

Where did we get the idea that children are innocent? "No one thought of them as innocent creatures," Darnton writes of the cultural attitudes of 18th-century France. Entire peasant families often huddled together in bed for warmth, including occasional livestock. The parents' sexual activities were frank, adjacent, upfront. "The child," as a social and biological category, simply didn't exist. Children were little farmhands, little servants, little apprentices. They were shorter, smaller, less effectual adults. "The peasants of early modern France," Darnton writes, "inhabited a world of stepmothers and orphans, of inexorable, unending toil, and of brutal emotions, both raw and repressed." The girl murdered by the wolf in the old folktale doesn't *deserve* her fate. She didn't disobey her mother; she didn't stray from the moral path. That's what makes the story so shocking. As Darnton puts it: "She simply walked into the jaws of death."

Many of the early modern French folktales seem sexual, scatological, and gratuitously violent, even to me, a kid raised on my mother's stories of Ted Bundy and a face-eating chimpanzee. Darnton recounts a number of peasant tales in *The Great Cat*

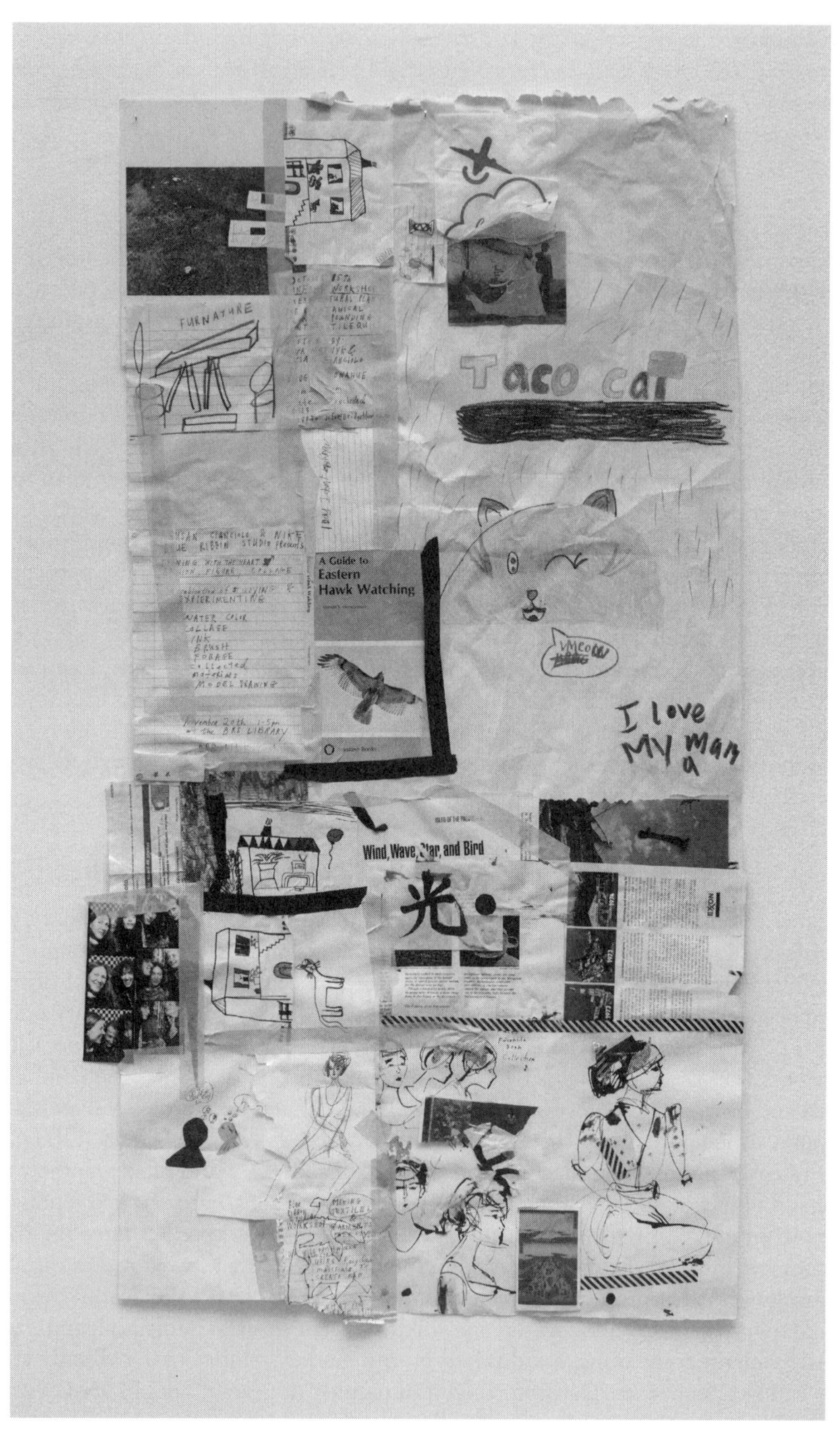

Susan Cianciolo, *Taco Cat*, 2017. Ink, graphite, crayon, glitter, photographs, tape, and collage on paper. 46 x 25 1/2 inches. Image courtesy of the Overduin & Co., Los Angeles

Massacre. In one of them, Persinette (the French Rapunzel) and the prince sew shut the anus of her pet parrot to keep the bird from tattling on the couple's sexual escapades in the tower. The preoccupied parrot can only croak: "Ass stitched. Ass stitched." In another tale, "La Poupée," an orphaned girl owns a magic toy that defecates gold when she commands: "Crap, crap, my little rag doll." When a neighbor steals her mini-Midas, the doll craps actual crap onto the thief and works its magic so that the neighbor's own turd clings to his anus and bites him. In "Ma mère m'a tué, mon père m'a mangé," a mother bakes a casserole made savory with chunks of her son's diced-up corpse, which her daughter in turn serves to the father. And in an early version of "Sleeping Beauty," Prince Charming rapes and impregnates the unconscious princess, who awakens from the spell when her nursing infants bite her breasts.

ᔓᔕ

Luna sat very still, her mind racing at what her own memory had revealed to her. Her own unlocked memory.

ᔓᔕ

"Although I am only fifteen," a girl I'll call Emma wrote to me, "your poems make me very nostalgic for the past." Her letter arrived about two weeks after I'd received Jodi's note. "I know that I personally think about my childhood in a positive light," Emma said, "but at the same time, thinking about the past makes me regret things I have done. It also makes me wonder how my past experiences have shaped who I am today, leading me to wonder if I even like the person I have become."

ᔓᔕ

She leaned forward and spat on the ground, making a small puddle of dusty mud. With her left hand she grabbed handful of dried grass, growing from a crack in the rock. She dipped it into the spittle-mud and started to wind it into a complicated knot.

ᔓᔕ

After my release from Dominion Hospital, I put a Wiccan curse on my ninth-grade algebra teacher, Mrs. Clarke, which involved the ritualistic tying of consecutive knots. (My stint as a runaway had lasted only a couple of nights.) Because I'd missed several weeks of class while hospitalized, I'd fallen behind in the lessons. I walked up to Mrs. Clarke's desk at the front of the room while the rest of the students worked on the in-class assignment. I pointed to an equation in my book and asked her for help. "Go ask your classmates," she said, glancing at my forearm blistered from elbow to wrist in cigarette burns. "They were here." I could feel my cheeks flare as I turned back toward my seat, the other students pretending not to see me.

The spell was simple. I'd picked the curse from my book on witchcraft because it didn't involve chicken blood or nude dancing in the woods. All I had to do was cut a length of string, tie a knot toward the bottom of it and say, "By knot of one, the spell's begun," while conjuring ill thoughts of my intended victim. I'd then add a second knot, an inch up from the first, and say: "By knot of two, it cometh true." And so forth ("By knot of three, let it be"), all the way up to 10. I don't recall how soon after the curse Mrs. Clarke's kitchen caught on fire while she was out shopping — I won't claim causality — but I do remember she was absent from class that spring for at least a week.

ഋര

"You asked me when I think childhood begins," I replied to Emma. "I probably have a better historical answer than a personal one." I wrote:

> We owe our contemporary perception of childhood (as a period of innocence, liberatory wonder, and creativity) first to the British Romantics of the late eighteenth century, such as Blake and Wordsworth, who drew from Rousseau's philosophy, and then to the Victorians, of the nineteenth century. Before that time, a more religious view, courtesy of the Puritans, dominated our ideas of children as sinful beings in need of strict moral guidance in a treacherous world — a pretty grim and paranoid notion.

I also addressed Emma's concern about whether or not she likes the person she's become. "Show me one person on this planet who likes *every* part of herself (especially a teenager)," I wrote. "She doesn't exist. I think realizing that we all contain parts that aren't flattering — that can be vindictive or jealous or selfish or small — is a natural part of maturity. Being perfect is, in addition to being impossible, pretty uninteresting."

ഋര

And inside the chrysalis, it changes. *Its body unmakes. Every portion of itself unravels, unwinds, undoes, and re-forms into something* else.

"What does it feel like?" Luna had asked.

"It feels like magic," her grandmother had said very slowly, her eyes narrowing.

ഋര

Cannibalism. Rape. Anus-biting turds. "If the world is cruel, the village nasty, and mankind infested with rogues," Darnton writes, "what is one to do?"

Although I'd laughed at Jodi's summary of my essays' subjects (*Serial killers! Hitler's genitalia! Anal rodent penetration!*) — reciting the trifecta in the cadences of an awestruck Dorothy (*Lions and tigers and bears, oh my!*) — I'd also recognized in the cannibalized book a much darker story. I saw in the cracked tale an allegory: a reflection of the way my optimism about Hillary Clinton's electoral chances in 2016 had suddenly split open to reveal the shocking and incongruous, a barbaric tear in the narrative.

What is it I'm looking for now, though, as I turn toward these old folktales? A brutal time that might remind me that we could be worse off? That we could be beaten-down, starving grunts on the bottom rung of feudal society? That any of us could walk into the jaws of death, unprepared, premature, undeservedly?

"The tales do not give an explicit answer," Darnton tells us, "but they illustrate the aptness of the ancient French proverb, 'One must howl with the wolves.'" Is that what we should do? Howl into the randomness, detached and ironic? Laugh at the swirling absurdities so as not to weep?

But oh! The sorrow hanging over the Protectorate!

And oh! The tyranny of grief!

The year that began in January 2017, with the new president's inauguration, ended that December, with the renal failure and euthanasia of my beloved cat. "It's what Michael Jackson OD'd on," the ER vet had said, waving that second syringe of breath-stopping medicine as she tried to — what? Comfort me? I hadn't realized I was a 37-year-old woman who secretly believed her black cat would live forever. Who assumed her stories would remain whole, bound tight, awaiting her there, right where she put them. I've been thinking that Trump becoming president is as grotesque and unlikely as my contributing serial killers and Hitler's scrotum to a best-selling children's book. After all, we don't always get an explanation when the story splits open. We must make like a peasant in a dark wood and howl with the wolves.

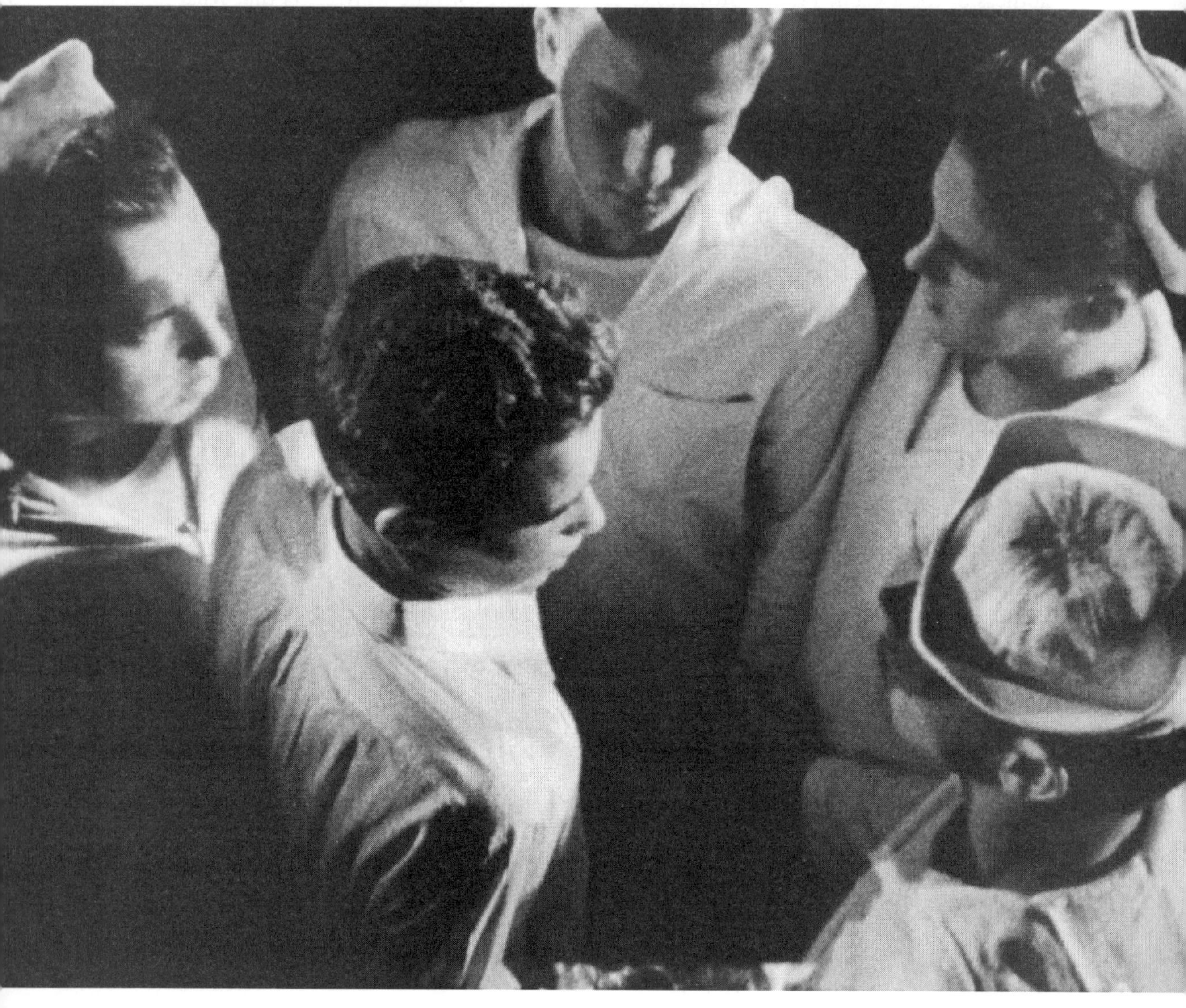

Opposite: Kenneth Anger, *Fireworks*, 1947. C-Print. 33 1/2 × 43 3/8 inches. Edition of 7

Above: Kenneth Anger, Harlequin *(Claude Revenant)*, 1950-73. C-Print. 33 1/2 × 43 1/8 inches. Edition of 7.

POSSUMS TELL ALL

FERNANDO A. FLORES

Whenever I visit back home and run into possums, I sometimes can't help myself and regress to a most primitive state. I start throwing rocks at the possums; stamp down one foot to scare them away. Make loud sounds very unlike actual words, just to add to the theater. Possums and myself, like all the other folks back home, have a difficult history. One time, straight out of high school, possums convinced us to enroll in a vocational class and learn to make air-conditioning ducts and shafts. A lot of air-conditioned buildings were popping up all over, they said. Somebody's gotta be making the ducts and shafts. Another time we skipped a whole month's worth of class to get stoned and drive around listening to the same records over and over. We'd kill a sixer driving up and down Jim Hogg County, singing out loud, smoking joints. It's strange to romanticize those difficult days, but here we are. I have to remind myself that possums were the ones spreading the rumor saying this land wasn't this land anymore; that this land was now *that* land. Even though you could be standing on this land you'd have to say, "I'm standing on *that* land," which belonged now to those over *there*. It took a few years for this to be straightened out, and by then everyone had forgot who started this confusion anyway. But a few of us remembered, and had to remind each other and ourselves every day, it was the possums started all this.

The possums laid low for a few years afterward — around the time kids started playing this rolling dice game and betting flowers in the streets. Soon, possums started writing and publishing tell-all books about one another, and people openly said, "Serves them right." Everyone read them, since each book was more cutting and revealing than the last. People lined up around the block on release days. Bookstores hadn't seen anything like it. A real phenomenon, everyone agreed. So now all is good with possums and the way of life back home.

ꕥ

Last time I was down for a visit I wandered off in the middle of the night and ended up at Perlitas Bar, where at a table by the jukebox blaring José José sat a possum, having a drink. I noticed a notebook where the possum was writing furiously. I asked if I could sit across the same table, and the possum nodded. For a while I just sat there reading my book, then after my second drink we got to talking — I stared into those eyes, like tiny stones dipped in ink, and as the night progressed the ink dripped out, and those eyes widened like a fault line in the ocean ripping open — from the fault emerged two hazy figures, like smoke out of an air shaft. The figures requested I follow them in, and inside the possum's eyes the dark, smoky figures and I had herbal tea. In the most polite manner, they suggested I tell nobody what I knew about possums. That it was in nobody's best interests to know. And, besides, everyone will find out soon enough — for there was a tell-all book about to be published that would recount everything that had transpired. When I asked the dark figures to elaborate they insisted they couldn't, for they were both under contract with the publishing company, and weren't at liberty to.

The following day I left the border, and since the possums ran their campaign and got elected, I have not returned.

Susan Cianciolo, *The Altar*, 2018. Wooden platform, cloth, paper, photographs, ink, safety pins, tape, and three drawings on paper. 85 x 145 1/2 x 68 inches. Image courtesy of the Overduin & Co., Los Angeles

UP IN THE AIR: CHARLES DURANT AND THE CLAIRVOYANTS

EMILY OGDEN

Amelia Andros's body sat in a rocking chair at the Varick House hotel in Manhattan. But her spirit traveled to Jersey City, to the home of balloonist Charles Ferson Durant. Durant was in the room with Andros and had suggested the destination of this supernatural visit. No sooner did Durant make his proposal than Andros replied, "I will fly there"; within seconds, she announced her arrival in his parlor. Andros then described things her bodily eyes had never seen: Durant's parlor furnishings, his carpet, and "*something strange, it looks like silk*" that was spread out upstairs. (It was one of Durant's balloons.)

Andros was a clairvoyant. Under the influence of mesmerism, a technique akin to hypnosis practiced in 1830s America, she entered a state of suspended animation known as *somnambulism*. Ordinary sensations in the here and now failed to reach her, but she could see distant places. She could also identify objects when blindfolded; it seemed that she saw out of spiritual eyes located somewhere near her diaphragm. Her husband William Andros was her mesmerist. They hailed from Providence, Rhode Island, and they had come to New York to give lectures showcasing Amelia's gifts. If successful, they would launch an East Coast tour.

Skeptics of mesmerism and somnambulism often came to these lectures to issue challenges. Durant, as a balloonist, considered himself a man of science, and so skepticism might have been expected of him. But after witnessing Andros's performance, he suddenly pronounced himself converted. Not only that, but he signed on to tour with the

Androses, even developing with them a theory of mesmerism's operations. He hypothesized that there was an invisible fluid that controlled sleep, wakefulness, sight, and volition. This fluid was thought to be similar to mineral magnetism, but it was associated with living beings. By "forcing a more than naturally rapid magnetic stream from the eye" — or in plain English, by staring at someone — you could place that person in a magnetic trance. "Strings or magnetic cords" would connect your eyes to the subject's mind. Along those cords, knowledge somehow traveled. Thus, when blindfolded clairvoyants saw what they could not have seen, or when spirit-voyagers knew what they could not have known, they were unwittingly reading the magnetist's mind. Clairvoyance, Durant argued, amounted to mind-reading. For more than a month, starting in August 1837, Durant traveled back and forth with the Androses (in the normal way, this time, on the steamer) between Providence and New York, excitedly promoting the magnetic cause. His friends became concerned. "Durant, I will bespeak for you a strait jacket, for I think you will want it soon," one well-wisher reportedly told him.

They need not have worried. Durant was conducting a sting operation. At that first visit to Amelia Andros, which he had undertaken on a bet, he detected her in fraud. The entranced Amelia claimed to see while blindfolded, but Durant was sure she peeped. The whole point of holding reading material at the diaphragm, he thought, was not that a spiritual eye was located there; it was that the clairvoyant could glance downward through the gap between the blindfold and her face. Her apparent voyages to unknown places were accomplished by a combination of acting skill, prior knowledge, and the ease with which common parlor furnishings could be guessed. In Durant's case, she would have known he was a balloonist; hence the "something strange, it looks like silk." As for his rug, she got lucky. Durant could have exposed her immediately, he wrote in *Exposition; or, A New Theory of Animal Magnetism*, the October 1837 best seller that revealed the fruits of his time undercover. But he thought he could do more to stop mesmerism's progress by countermining it from within. He "saw thousands of credulous people led astray," and he worried that "millions [...] would in all probability become dupes to the deception" if something was not done. So he imitated an earnest investigator, sifting the evidence for various theories, feigning belief in certain aspects of the performance and performing his suspicion about others. "I must not be a believer in *all* the effects, but must leave *some* effects to dispute with the professors," he wrote, "in order to elicit experiments from each subject." He believed that what was true of the Androses, was true of most magnetizer-somnambulist pairs: the magnetizers, generally men, "knew nothing of the secret; they were honest and sincere in their pretensions." The somnambulists — the women — were the charlatans.

Along with Andros, about a half-dozen other women are recorded as having traveled in spirit during the summer and fall of 1837. Most were based in Providence, a city that the writer James Freeman Clarke called the "head quarters" of mesmerism in America. Providence, a leading industrial center that produced cotton textiles and the machines textile factories used, had risen to mesmeric prominence in part by luck. US mesmerism's founder, Charles Poyen, and its first great clairvoyant, textile factory worker Cynthia Gleason, first encountered each other in Providence. As their collaboration took off in the winter of 1836, Providence's citizens responded by forming magnetizer-clairvoyant pairs, documenting somnambulistic experiments, and submitting the chronically ill to mesmeric cures. American mesmerism spread outward from this node of intense activity, of which the Androses were part. Both of the Androses also had industry connections. Amelia was the daughter of a cotton factory owner, and William manufactured varnish.

Cotton tied Providence to the national and global economy. Baled cotton arrived in the factories from Southern plantations that enslaved men, women, and children. Trade wars with England had a material effect on textile industrialists' profits. The capital that sustained the whole system came from New York and New Orleans. In the summer of 1837, the liabilities of such ties were especially apparent. The peak of experimentation in traveling somnambulism came only a few months after the catalytic event of that year's great depression: the cascading collapse of New Orleans and New York financial markets known as the Panic of 1837. For investors in Providence textile factories, knowing what was coming just a little bit earlier than everyone else did could have made a significant difference to their losses. Might somnambulists have offered the manufacturers of Providence that critical edge? One newspaper editor hopefully suggested that they could provide advanced warning of shifting cotton prices in southern markets. As a practical matter, somnambulists did not engage in corporate espionage; they were much more likely to visit tourist destinations. But however prosaic its usual forms, somnambulism played into a fantasy of omniscience that was particularly powerful in this age of economic uncertainty. If only one could know the bad news before anyone else, maybe there would be some chance of protecting oneself.

Traveling somnambulism was one of a number of developing communication technologies that promised to offer a leg up. If genuine, somnambulism would have been the fastest means of either communication or locomotion available anywhere in the world. Durant called it a technique for "annihilating distance." At the time, Samuel F. B. Morse was developing the electromagnetic telegraph, but no infrastructure yet existed to support it. The Napoleonic Empire boasted a semaphore system by which signals could be relayed from hill to hill, at six-mile intervals, with coded pulses of a beacon; remarkable as this imperial feat was, the beacon system was still slower than Andros. Most news traveled with human beings, carried by trains, steamboats, or horses. Not that those forms of conveyance would have seemed slow at the time: dramatic improvements in transportation infrastructure over the previous 20 years meant that Americans were living in an age whose sense of mediated expansiveness — of uncertain possibility and risk — somewhat resembles our own. Still, speed begat the desire for speed. Annihilate distance, and you could coin money.

In his own professional life, Durant had bet on a different horse, so to speak: not spirit-travel, but ballooning. Durant was not alone in thinking that the balloon was the next steam ship. In Edgar Allan Poe's futuristic tale "Mellonta Tauta" (1849), ordinary travelers of the coming age hop aboard a balloon built to carry a crowd. "Aerostation," or balloon travel, dated back to the late 18th century in France, but it was only about a decade old in the United States. Durant was a pioneer in the field. On one occasion, some 20,000 people watched him ascend from Manhattan's Battery in a green silk balloon festooned with colored ribbons and decorated with a portrait of DeWitt Clinton, the popular former governor who had spearheaded the Erie Canal (another distance-bridging technological feat that had transformed the movement of goods between the northeast and the interior). Durant tossed out souvenir copies of a poem called "The Aeronaut's Address" as he ascended. "Goodbye to you, people of earth / I am soaring to regions above you," the poem announced. Durant skated over Staten Island, shouting to the inhabitants as he passed, before touching down at Perth Amboy, New Jersey.

These amusements concealed serious purpose. If balloon travel could be perfected, it might revolutionize transatlantic commerce, reducing the trip from England to America to a few days. Several years before publishing his story about aerotravel, Poe perpetrated his "Balloon Hoax." The piece was first published in the *New York Sun* in April 1844 and purported to be a dispatch from Charleston, South Carolina, where the first transatlantic balloon flight had just landed. (Actually, a balloon did not cross the Atlantic until the *Double Eagle II* made the trip in 1978.) The story came out in an extra of the *Sun*, set in type just as though it were a news account and timed to appear between the arrival of two mail deliveries from Charleston. Accounts of the hoax's reception vary, but it seems likely that for at least a few hours, people believed. Here was yet another argument for the urgency of annihilating distance: in the interval between the mails, there was no way to check whether a dispatch was true. The land mass holding Charleston could have cleaved off from the mainland and fallen into the ocean without anyone in New York being the wiser. A traveling somnambulist, on the other hand, could have pierced Poe's illusion almost instantly, by spiriting herself down to Charleston and checking things out.

It's at least possible that professional rivalry inspired Durant's investigation into traveling somnambulism. Here was a technology that, if real, would easily surpass his own preferred futuristic mode of flight. In his book, Durant reserved for special ridicule a comparison that another mesmerism investigator made between ballooning and traveling somnambulism. Like Durant, William Leete Stone, prominent editor of the *New York Commercial Advertiser*, had approached mesmerism as a skeptical investigator. But unlike him, Stone converted to the cause. In Stone's *Letter to Doctor A. Brigham, on Animal Magnetism* (1837), published just weeks before Durant's *Exposition*, he breathlessly described how the blind clairvoyant Loraina Brackett spirit-traveled to New York under his guidance. When somnambulists voyaged, a visitor often narrated their progress to them as a way of guiding them to a particular place. Such a person might suggest following the railway line to Roxbury, or turning right on Broadway. Thus even though the travel was spiritual, somnambulists and their visitors imagined their itineraries with striking specificity. On Stone's visit, he suggested to Brackett that they should fly to

EXPERIMENT IN ANIMAL MAGNETISM.

Cerin (or tissue paper) scattering the "will" of the Magnetizer to prevent somnambulism. *Vide Chapter XIV.*

New York in an (imaginary) balloon, saying that he was "used to that way of traveling." Durant's pride was perhaps offended by this cavalier claim to ballooning expertise: he repeats this scene with a great many scare quotes, exclamation points, and italicized words. Durant, after all, was far better qualified to say he was "used to that way of traveling" than Stone was.

After several weeks of cordial participation in Amelia Andros's experiments, Durant decided the time had come to spring his trap. He took Amelia aside and told her that he had made a secret discovery. While the magnetic fluid that allowed Amelia to "travel" into people's minds or faraway places could pass through walls and travel great distances, there was one substance that stopped it: "CERIN, an animal fat which was discovered in a graveyard, where dead bodies had been buried for many years." Durant claimed that by blocking the magnetist's gaze with cerin-soaked paper, he could prevent magnetism from working. The paper would prevent the magnetic cords from forming, which would prevent communication between mesmerist and clairvoyant.

The true purpose of this ruse was to show that it was up to Amelia to decide whether or not mental magnetism would work. There was no such thing as cerin, nor was there any reason to think that the magnetic bonds, if they existed, would be impeded by animal fat. What mattered were Amelia Andros's convictions. If she thought that the success of the experiment depended upon her *not* being magnetized, her husband's efforts would have no effect. Durant's experimental design closely resembled a well-known early debunking of mesmerism in Paris, by Benjamin Franklin, Antoine Lavoisier, and a committee of other scientists. Franklin's team had shown that subjects were affected when they believed they were being mesmerized — even if nothing was actually happening. And they had shown subjects to be unaffected when they were mesmerized without their knowledge. The Franklin group thought subjects were sincere but affected by the powers of suggestion. Durant minced no words: he took Amelia to be a fraud.

Durant then performed the experiment: Amelia was in on the "secret" of the cerin-soaked paper, but William Andros was still in the dark. Durant asked William to magnetize Amelia from across town at a pre-appointed time — a feat the trio had successfully performed many times before. The idea in the past had been to prove that magnetism worked at a distance. Now, the idea was to prove that it didn't work at all — unless Amelia wanted it to work. At the agreed-upon time, Durant held up the sheet of "cerin" to Amelia's face. Nothing happened. Amelia did not go into a state of clairvoyance, did not travel, and did not experience anything out of the ordinary. When William returned to the hotel, Durant and Amelia brought him up to speed. In Durant's representation, the Androses were thrilled to be the first to know about this newly discovered property of mesmeric power. Cerin was the magnetizer's Kryptonite. Durant pretended to be thrilled, too: "Nothing could now delay the lectures, and an immense fortune would soon be acquired by both of us," he wrote. "Both" means him and William; as he often does, Durant casually counts Amelia out.

The "beautiful experiment," as Durant satirically called it, was a brilliant success on another level, too: it permitted Durant to begin unraveling his web of deception and preparing for the publication of the *Exposition*. His plan was to disabuse the Providence mesmerizers who were then in New York of their false belief in their clairvoyants, including the Androses and also two other magnetists recently arrived from Providence, William Grant and Americus Potter. He intended for the *Exposition* to be a shot across all their bows: they would have time to cancel their lecture tours and slink back to Providence with at least a little bit of their dignity intact.

But before Durant could intervene, Grant and Potter advertised public lectures at the Clinton Hotel. And so he perpetrated a final hoax designed to countermand the notion that "immense fortunes" were being acquired at the expense of a credulous public. The banking system of the United States was then in turmoil, with Western banks issuing their own currency whose value could hardly be determined day to day. If a bank went belly up, its notes became worthless, but news of these busts traveled slowly and unevenly. That meant it was sometimes possible to pass broken bank notes to unsuspecting recipients. Durant now orchestrated a scheme where a crowd of plants would buy all the tickets to the Grant-Potter lectures with broken bank notes. Tickets would sell but would be purchased with worthless money. This ruse would also prevent magnetists from saying later, "well, if it is all deception, New York helped to pay for it." He then disillusioned William Andros, telling him that his wife had perhaps started out trying to be sincere, but eventually, she had "feigned the whole." To Amelia he had, apparently, nothing to say. Durant's *Exposition* appeared to much fanfare in early October. It was a "perfect scorcher," said a Buffalo, New York, paper. The first edition sold out in less than a week (though Providence booksellers loyally refused to carry it). The *Boston Post* called Durant a "master of human nature."

It might be tempting to praise Durant for having the common sense to see that up is up, and down is down. Yet there are strong reasons to pause before signing up for his fan club. Misogyny fueled his crusade against clairvoyance. His general view was that conniving women had made idiots of their honest, but too trusting, male mesmerists. Amelia Andros sought attention, he thought. Another clairvoyant, Ann Eliza Ebon, liked having men paw at her. He called Brackett "insipid, immodest, vulgar, and disgusting" and accused her of feigning blindness to shirk labor. No wonder there were rumors that a group of clairvoyants planned to sue him for libel. It's unclear whether that lawsuit ever went forward, but the mesmeric community did take other forms of revenge. A "lady Phrenologist" performing as "Miss Martha" advertised her clairvoyant skills under the heading, "Defeat of Mr. Durant." She illustrated her poster with a decidedly flaccid-looking balloon.

There's another big problem with the image of Durant as a gimlet-eyed rationalist. He seems to have written the first 50 pages of what later became the *Exposition* in a state of sincere belief. As one reviewer put it, these four chapters are "taken up with an unnecessarily prolix and rambling statement of [his] 'theory,' and the reader will be very apt upon a perusal of this portion of the book, to suppose the writer a believer himself." It's true: these chapters seem for all the world to have been written by someone who is actually proposing a new mesmeric doctrine. Durant promises to offer a theory of traveling somnambulism, which, he says, is "the most extraordinary feature of the science," and yet it had not been theorized: "it remains unaccounted for [...] in this country or elsewhere." Durant seems far too anxious to sell readers on the unique strengths of his theory, as when he makes the promise that he will teach people how to self-mesmerize. Such a promise is somewhat unusual in mesmerists' texts in this period, and it seems to betray a certain investment in theoretical innovation. He also downplays the impact of Benjamin Franklin's 1784 debunking of mesmerism — the very investigation on which his own technique of trapping clairvoyants with a sham device, the cerin-soaked paper, was clearly based — although in the preface, which was apparently written last, he praises Franklin to the skies.

Durant foresaw that there might be "some objections" to these chapters and claimed they were parodic: "[T]he best satire on a false doctrine is to award it *all* the attributes which its deluded votaries claim for their idol." Maybe. But here's an alternate explanation. Durant first met the Androses in August, and by early October, his more than 200-page book was in the hands of booksellers. Durant must have written like the wind. He may even have been giving pages to his publisher to set in type as he finished them. Why not explain the oddities of that opening section by imagining that it was written in good faith, and then repurposed later when Durant became disillusioned — and when there was too little time, or energy, to start all over at the beginning?

In that case Durant's rage against magnetism was the fury of the apostate — and perhaps also the fury of the aspiring popular-scientific author who had written some 50 pages in animal magnetism's defense that could now be salvaged only with difficulty. It may be that his elaborate mousetrap for Amelia Andros was baited not with feigned belief, but with genuine belief freshly killed.

The truth is that feigned belief is not as easy to distinguish from credulity as one might like to imagine. Durant himself makes this point when describing Amelia Andros's state of mind during her animal-magnetic experiments. He sums up by saying that she "feigned the whole," but in the details he allows that things were more complicated than that. He imagines that William first was "led to believe" because he saw that other people, whom he thought of as more intelligent or better informed than himself, believed. Then Amelia saw William's "infatuation" and "very naturally humored the delusion; she even probably supposed the science was true." Believing, she "was not capable of scanning her feelings; she felt a queer sensation, and she supposed it must be magnetism." Eventually, because she "wished to please" her husband, and because she was "fond of fame," she undertook to deceive in earnest.

How different are these gradations of feigned and real belief from the best account we can form of Durant's own trajectory? If Durant was inclined to credit mesmerism at first, when he knew little about it, then he, too, had been "led to believe" by the beliefs of others. The ambiguities of the *Exposition*'s first four chapters show their writer oscillating between belief and doubt before finally settling on a feigned belief at least as elaborate as Amelia Andros's own — if indeed Durant was right about her state of mind. And as for being "fond of fame," a man who carefully choreographed the launch of a decorated balloon in front of 20,000 people surely couldn't cast aspersions.

It is not always easy to determine our own beliefs, let alone the beliefs of others. Durant's poisonous misogyny may have been a way of projecting onto women a weakness of his own that he did not want to countenance: he, too, was capable of playing along, feigning, losing his way. He, too, was vulnerable to deception. And here is what's suspect about debunking. Right or wrong, debunkers' work generally carries a pronounced benefit for them personally, by casting them as the rational ones. Debunkers are often right. But even when they're wrong, they gain at least this much: so long as they are occupied in pointing out the illusions of others, they don't have to think about their own.

FROM WEST TEXAS

MATT MORTON

The javelina crossed the interstate soundtracked by Satie's Gnossienne 2.

"To the northwest of us is a firing range, do not be alarmed at the sounds of."

There was no trail. A tiny family on the summit.

Oil derricks pecking rhythmically at the earth on this our day of thanks.

I wear a pair of old brown boots and my father's jacket.

The population of Alpine dips below 6,000 in accordance with the season.

Suspicion that this world is a collection of seemings, a mixed bag.

My hand reaches for hers in the rented dark.

See the impression of the wind on sagebrush?

Fields of bunchgrass, hoofprints like crescent moons in the sand.

As context shifts so too identity, as in the case of a windmill placed on the bottom of the ocean.

Yucca, juniper, caliche. Like a prepared Turner canvas, the pastel bands of sky.

So tentative each carefully weighted step from stone to stone.

"The source of the ghost lights remains unknown to this day."

Inside the bookshop a girl describes a kestrel, her voice is a wind chime.

Belief I conceal from most people I love that the absence of form will assume a shape.

There are two churches in town and three service stations.

After sundown even the Milky Way must work up the courage.

Election signs wait at the edge of private property.

In his later work, the foreground figures merge with the atmosphere.

What passes here for mountains.

For three years, this famine of the spirit.

When I run out of medicine my experience of the desert sharpens, but I become lost in it.

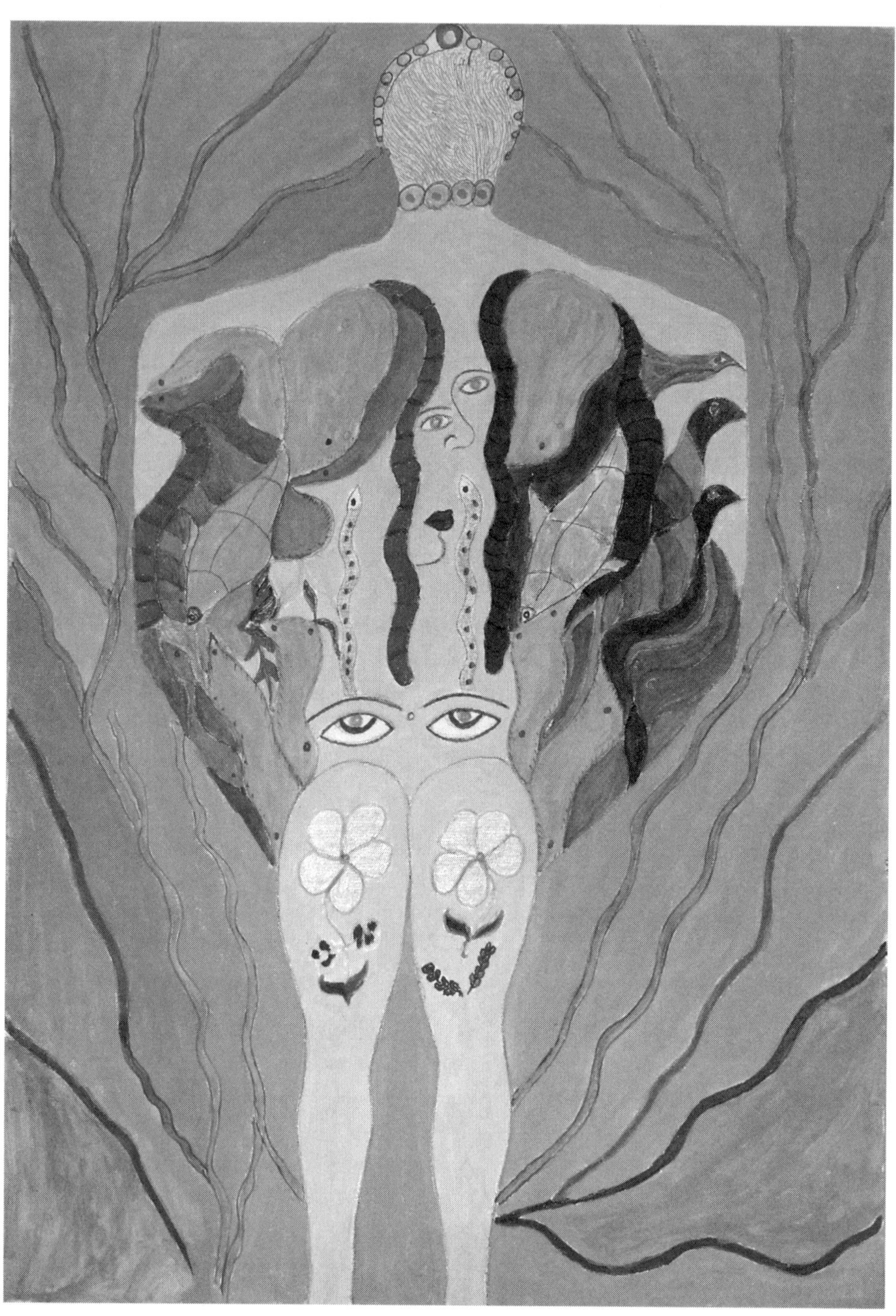

Reza Shafahi, *Untitled*, 2015. Acrylic & marker on paper. 50 x 70 cm. Image courtesy of the artist

THE LINDOW MAN

SARAH MOSS

I met my first bog person when I was nine.

I grew up in Manchester, a post-industrial city in northwest England, which is now rather fashionable but in the 1980s was just poor and violent and getting poorer and more violent. Manchester's infrastructure and most of the buildings are Victorian, built with pomp and confidence in the years when cotton and corn money was pouring into the city from across the Empire. There's a grand museum, made in the 19th century to display both colonial loot and new industrial technologies for which northern England was then famous. The museum was an obvious wet-weather outing and, Manchester being famously rainy, we went often. I knew the snakes in the vivaria, their low-ceilinged room one of few places I felt warm in winter, and the sparkly rocks in the glass cases upstairs. There were stuffed animals, some of them extinct but nonetheless accommodated with branches to climb and stones underfoot, and there were the skeletons of whale strung up like chandeliers and a dinosaur reaching up to snuff their ribcages. (A scent on the air like our "wax crayons" which were still made of whale fat.) I remember a family of crocodiles living behind glass, actually alive, moving sometimes sulkily from backstage into their shallow pond, real water surrounded by droopy plants. But surely that can't be right, can it, there can't have been live crocodiles on the second floor of a Victorian museum in the city center? There was, for sure, a large collection of Egyptian mummies, past which I had to be led with my eyes closed because if I saw their flaking toes and eyeless faces they would creep into my mind and come out in my bedroom at night, take skinny form in the coffin-sized space between my bed and the wall, come scratching their ancient fingernails against my rattling Victorian window, signal their watching presences in the clanking of our ineffectual Victorian radiators. The museum is on the main bus route into Manchester from the south and every time I passed it, I remembered the mummies lying there, arms folded like impatient teachers, just a few feet from the rush-hour traffic and the street lights and the rain.

One day there was a new presence in the museum, and my class had a school trip to mark the occasion. We'd all heard the story: someone digging for peat in Lindow Moss, a bog just south of the city, had turned up a dead body. Seeing a human leg in his digger's scoop, Andy Mould (yes, really) naturally called the police, who soon called the archaeologists. The body was that of a young man who had died around the time of Christ. He had multiple injuries, several of them sufficient to cause death: a blow to the head with something like an axe, a chest wound, a broken neck, and a ligature of sinew tightly around his neck. He was small by modern standards, about five feet and seven inches and 135 pounds, but in good health, suffering only the gut parasites normal for most people in most of human time. He was well groomed and manicured and had had a meal of grains and flatbreads shortly before death. Exposed to human gaze for the first time in two millennia, Lindow Man spent some time in the mortuaries of local hospitals before being transferred to London for investigation, and apart from occasional visits to the city of his birthplace, London is where he has stayed. Lindow Man lives in the British Museum now, but his first audience since his violent death was in Manchester, in our museum.

Bodies are found in bogs across northern Europe, often bearing the marks of deliberate injury. Peat bogs preserve skin, tan it and dye hair red, and in doing so hold the stories of people who left no words. In places where peat has been used as fuel, the discovery of the ancient dead was frequent enough that even in the 18th century, peasant farmers knew to notify the pastor who often enough contacted the universities in the capital cities of Denmark, Sweden, and Ireland. We sometimes know how but never why Iron Age Europeans killed members of their communities and left them in bogs, sometimes in quite complicated arrangements; some bog bodies were staked down, as if to stop them rising again, or left surrounded by strange objects. We do know that important possessions were often deliberately broken and placed in bogs. Archaeologists think of sacrifice, an old set of beliefs about the hinterlands of water and earth that we've inherited in the habit of throwing coins into wells and fountains. People bent jeweled and inlaid swords, cut off braids of hair, damaged beautiful and expensive musical instruments and laid them in swamps. In some places, piers and walkways were built out over the shallow water, perhaps for ritual purposes ("ritual purposes" often means "we can imagine no practical reason for this course of action," which doesn't mean there wasn't a practical reason in the Iron Age).

The historical record of northern Europe begins with the arrival (or invasion) of the Romans, who, like every imperial force in history, noted the tendency of the local savages to engage in human sacrifice. The Romans won and therefore so did their version of history, but recent scholars have suggested that some of the bog people may merely have gotten lost and fallen in, as many travelers did until modern maps marked footpaths and danger zones. Others may have been victims of common or garden murder, their bodies just evidence handily concealed in the bog. Many of the injuries may be post-mortem and, in some cases, caused by the removal of the body from the bog, but none of these sensible theories explains all the evidence. As an archaeologist pointed out to me, if it was so easy to fall into bogs and drown, one would expect to find the remains of other mammals too, but there are very few animal bog bodies. The bog people include a disproportionate number with disabilities and birth defects, who would have differed from most of their contemporaries in appearance, gait, and physical abilities, although almost all reached adulthood in adequate health. This was not form of euthanasia. There are similarities in the ways of killing and arranging bodies between Denmark, England, and Ireland that seem unlikely to be coincidental and suggest an understanding of method, if not necessarily motive shared across the seas.

I don't remember making any wider study of bog bodies then. I think my teachers wanted us to be excited about the new technologies that brought us detailed information about this Iron Age individual. There was also some local pride in an event that had global media attention, especially in a city better known for modern murder. Maybe the exhibit did inspire some young scientists, but for me it was about violence and horror seeping out of my own landscape. My interest in archaeology is life-long and I've always been particularly intrigued by Iron Age Europe, the last years of prehistory before the Romans brought writing to Europe's northern fringe. Even then, I loved Iron Age hill forts and barrows, enjoyed the sense of brushing fingertips with people from the deep past who left us no words, but I didn't want to see their skin and flesh in my own time and place. I was, I see now, ambivalent about my own body, aware of its porousness and fragility and capacity for pain. I had no faith or ontology to make death anything other than frightening and final, and I couldn't understand how people who knew that death was coming could avoid thinking about it. Archaeology, I suppose, gave me a kind of faith, in the continuity of human experience, in the durability of the work of human hands, in the constancy of landscape.

I did look at Lindow Man, and he looked simultaneously human and inhuman, his shrivelled nakedness and exposed wounds an indecent display of inanimation. This is all we are in the end — surfaces, husks, membranes between blood and air. I looked at his broken limbs and torn skin, his open mouth and closed eyes, and in his brokenness he didn't haunt me the way the neatly laid out Egyptian mummies did. I didn't want to see him — still don't, much — but for pity, not for fear.

Raha Raissnia, *Galvanoscope 1*, 2018. Projector, 16mm film, wood, scrim, 3 min. loop. Sculpture dimensions: 23 x 31 x 31 inches.
Overall installation dimensions variable. Edition of 2 + 1 AP. Courtesy of the artist and Miguel Abreu Gallery, New York. Photo: Stephen Faught

THE RETREAT

KEZIAH WEIR

His room at the retreat was in the roof of the old barn. The main part of the farm building, which once housed horses, was used mostly for storage, now, and the two therapy mares left on the property lived on the other side of the big field in a newer, smaller stable.

His rooms, rather, because it was really three stacked one in front of the other, railroad style. Bedroom, kitchen, office, with what they quaintly used to call a water closet in one corner, a little bathroom with no sink or shower. They smelled, still, of hay and cedar, and Henry felt when he entered them as though some great weight was being lifted from his shoulders. Here, he could finally write, unencumbered by the troubling preoccupations he'd left behind in Manhattan. His laptop was open on the hewn-wood work table — the only piece of furniture in the northernmost room, save for a Shaker chair — awash in light from the window that looked out on the back of the property, the unmown fields and celadon woods beyond. He disconnected from the internet following a momentary irritation that there was even internet to be had, and turned off his phone, dropping it in the bottom drawer of the dresser.

Henry made these quick preparations while Norah chatted at him, opening the window to "let the air in" along with the shushing metallic hum of summer insects, supplying the history of the Center and how the artist residency had come about — rich dying donor — and the various available programs and amenities free to the artists during their stay. Sweat lodge sessions, nighttime meditations, emotional narrative building, whatever that meant, neural firing scans, all things of which Henry knew he would not be availing himself. His girlfriend had mentioned some of these details, too, reading from the Center's website the week before he left, and he'd glazed over. He was there to write.

He'd taken the subway, then a two-hour bus ride upstate, and then a half-hour cab. At first, after Norah met him at the fork in the dirt road where the taxi dropped him off, and walked him through the sprawling property; after she'd brought him into the cool dark barn and led him up the stairs through the golden dust motes, he'd felt a twinge of annoyance that she didn't abscond immediately, leaving him alone with his thoughts. But as she chirped away about the secretive, cultish group that had occupied the property years before the Center moved in and all the paraphernalia they'd left behind, a Ouija board and half-burned books of strange symbols, he was grateful for the patter, not ready to be alone in his mind quite yet. Her presence was familiar, the way his wife used to sit on the bedroom floor when he packed for reporting trips, and his mother helped him clean his room as a child. Norah was leaning against the desk, almost sitting on it with her hands in the pockets of her butter yellow jumpsuit. She was his age, maybe a little younger. Early 30s, with a milk-fed farmgirl ease. He could easily imagine her naked. Firmly long and round all over. She talked about the founding of the Center in the '80s, her father's work, which he shared with his wife — not Norah's mother, Henry gathered. Positron emission tomography, she said, brain scans, a program that promoted creativity and self-knowledge by coupling hard science with something called dreamwork. Not Freudian, obviously, she assured him.

"During the scan they make a series of statements about the subject and her work. The sections of the brain that become illuminated can reveal subconscious thought. Answers the person didn't know she had."

"Like a truth machine," he said, locating a glass in a cabinet and running the tap.

"Kind of. Oh, it'll be rusty. Totally safe, just a little off-putting." The water, indeed, was a reddish brown. "Just let it go for a couple minutes first. He does the scan for other people too, not just artists, but people trying to make big decisions. It takes you out of yourself. One woman, this kind of powerbitch finance lady, she was married and having an affair and she wanted to know if she should leave her husband."

The tap water was starting to run clear. Henry filled his glass, held it up to the light and watched the pale particles of decay settle into the bottom. He drank.

"So dad hooked her up and asked her these questions designed to elicit different responses. The neocortical activity in the amygdala went insane. The areas associated with sadness lit up like a bonfire. But it was *past* sadness, sadness for something that no longer existed. Basically the woman was already mourning her lover because she'd decided, though she didn't know it yet, that she was going to stay with her husband, who she didn't love."

"Wow," he said. "This is all proven? Peer reviewed, all that?"

"The brain stuff is. The rest of the program is more—" she shrugged.

"Sure. And you live on the property?"

"Oh, god no. That's funny. No, I live in Williamsburg. I'm in PR. You know that yoga studio on North 7th? I live above there. I just come up to make sure dad and Ray aren't burning the place down. Filing tax forms. You know. They might be brilliant and enlightened, but they're disorganized as hell. I was trying to go over their wills this weekend but Ray's in the last days of one of her fasts. Not ideal. Anyway," she straightened up. "If you have everything you need, I'll leave you be. I should get back to the city."

"Okay," he said. "Thanks."

"You're lucky, I think this is the nicest room in the compound," she said as she started down the ladder. "Supposedly they used it for séances. Some people say lost souls still converge around here on hot nights, out by the trees. Singing siren songs that drive the listener mad. Maybe you'll be visited by a spirit. Maybe she'll whisper an ending into your ear." She laughed, a benevolent little hissing noise like an air leak. So it was a joke, then. "Dinner's at seven in the main building. Big one on the left. Good luck with your novel."

And then he was alone. He walked from the office through to the bedroom, listening to the boards creak, breathing in the soft sweet air. On a beam above the doorless office doorway there were words carved in: Ludibrio me adhuc habuisti. He wrote them down in his notebook to look up later. He did a couple push-ups next to the desk, sat down, woke up the computer, laid his fingers on the keyboard, took them off, sat back, stared outside.

He had taken himself away from his life so he could work in quiet, prompted by an incident that had occurred a couple weeks earlier. That morning, following months of a block, he had just begun to formulate a fledgling idea. He was sitting at his desk in the corner of the living room and his girlfriend was periodically reading passages from some article about Sylvia Plath, and the mention of that woman, whose writing his wife had loved, was so distracting that it knocked out any creative possibility. Suddenly he was standing up and the cup he'd been holding was broken on the floor, in the corner of the room. Hot coffee was streaking the wall. His girlfriend was nowhere near the accident, but she was staring at him with something like confusion and something like terror — terror, Jesus, toward him! — and he had stopped himself from whatever else he might have said and went into the bedroom to cool down, and when he came out the mug and coffee were cleaned up, and when he said he thought he should go away for a few weeks to the program upstate that she (that is, I) had mentioned earlier that week, if there were any spots left, she'd looked relieved and happy and had hugged him around his neck and kissed his cheek and said she thought (that is, I thought) that sounded like a wonderful idea, it would be great to get away, he'd been working so hard, and he said this would be for work too. And now here he was, working. He *would* work.

A few hours later he walked through the fields to the hall where dinner was served. A dozen other people were there already eating quietly. Mealtime, he'd read in the pamphlet Norah left him, could be used for quiet introspection or the positive exchange of ideas. They just had one resident artist at a time, so the other people were mostly permanent fixtures, she'd explained, people with brain injuries or psychological trauma who had sought treatment from her father and his wife Ray and never left. They built their own small houses across the 80 acres owned by the Center, and contributed by keeping trails clear, maintaining the campsites, cooking for the short-term visitors who paid for the week- and month-long programs the Center coordinated several times a year. It was all more hippie-dippy than he'd expected, but it was fine, it was quiet, and it was not Manhattan. After dinner, having talked to no one, Henry walked back to the barn through the fields, the sky just starting to glow pink and lavender, and sat back down at the desk, watching the dark descend.

He hadn't spent a night alone, he realized, since he'd gone to the apartment three days after Lily died. He hadn't lived there for months — he had another place to stay — but it was as though no time had passed for either of them. Could it be that the bed still held the imprint of her body? Or was it a trick of the light? So many people had offered to go before him, to clean things up before he arrived, and he should have let them, though at the time it had seemed inconceivable that someone else should touch the things she last touched, that he should never again see the eye cream in the refrigerator, the slippers beside the bed, the solitary movie ticket — some glossy big budget thing she'd asked him to go to and he'd brushed off — that she'd used to mark her place in the book on her nightstand. He thumbed through the pages, saw something about violating the secret of the pharaohs, put it aside.

She had accumulated so many things, his wife, bits of paper, old calendars, vinyl records, Playbills, museum maps. If they'd thrown them out, before, together, it would have been cleaning; now, to do so seemed sacrilegious. So he just left it until the apartment sold. She had no parents, but there were friends who wanted clothing, jewelry, bits of her. And then there were black trash bags. He kept one small filing box, which he moved from the top reaches of his expansive new closet (my family has always been generous with me), then to under the bed, and finally into the bottom drawer of his desk, where he kept tax documents, and where his girlfriend would never need to look. He put some of Lily's books back onto his shelves. Her wedding ring was buried with her.

But he didn't want to think about Lily. He climbed into bed, lay staring up into the black. It was so dark, and the noises outside were strange, hypernatural. No cars, no horns. For a long time, he tried to make out what sounded like a distant human voice floating over the fields, some unknown ghostly neighbor, what, reciting a poem? Singing a song? Or two identical voices, maybe, saying goodnight. There was a scuffling of animals, the patter of small feet above his head, something gnawing, gnawing, tiny teeth chewing away, working to destroy the integrity of the house, not a house, the barn, the roof of the barn that had been abandoned but for him, those teeth going all through the night like little saws.

⁂

It's so easy to imagine him there among the pines. I've lived with him for over a year and in that time, we've hardly been apart, and even when we were strangers to each other and slowly became less so, it was like our lives had been waiting to entangle. It wouldn't have happened, otherwise, everything between us, I wouldn't have just thrown myself at any man. I was an assistant editor at his publisher, and we'd met in the lobby. I never met Lily. Nothing happened, physically, between us until he left her. When it finally did, my best friend was shocked. "You're so young, though. And now he's left his wife and everything's just going to be breezy?" I didn't know. But I thought so. In the beginning, for the first couple weeks, we did go slowly, getting to know each other shyly across tables and side by side as we walked through Central Park, but then we went to bed one Sunday evening and after that were more or less living together almost before I realized what was happening.

I knew what Lily looked like, of course, through the internet and the one Saturday morning — before Henry and I started seeing each other but after we'd established a flirtation — when, not proudly, I went to the cafe across from their apartment and waited until they came out together. She was striking, a poet with deep auburn hair and pale strange eyes and an otherwise unremarkable face. She was thin, too, very thin in the photographs. I conjured her hourly. During intimate moments, I had to remind myself not to think of her.

He'd told me things about their relationship. Some I wished he hadn't. One night when they were still living together they got into one of their shrieking fights, with her hurling things at his head because of some slight and him stalking uselessly around the room — what could he do, hit a woman? — and then she'd left and hadn't come home until late the next day; he could only imagine where she'd ended up. Sometimes she disappeared for days, a week. When they first started dating, a few months in, she'd gone into his bathroom one morning and come out with blood on her hand and a towel around her waist and said she thought she was having a miscarriage. Years later, she told him she was pregnant and then, after waiting for him to respond, as though administering a test, told him that the abortion was scheduled for later that week. She stopped writing poetry and started reading books she'd liked in college that he thought she'd grown out of: Sylvia Plath, Daphne du Maurier, Virginia Woolf, Clarice Lispector. She kept asking him to go to a witch shop downtown, and finally went on her own, spending an insane amount of money on crystals, rune books, tarot reading instructional classes, incense that stunk up the apartment, and then that place didn't feel real enough to her, it was so commercial, the people who came in were so often shopping for birthday presents, so she found a place in Queens and came back looking dazed and smelling of ash. In the middle of the night he would find her in a pool of candlelight at the kitchen table, hunched over the tarot deck. You don't really believe in this, though, right? He'd asked. You understand that the answers you think you're getting from this deck of cards are just your own interpretation, that you read into them basically what you want them to say. You don't believe in, well, magic. Or contact with the dead. Or a spirit world. Or—. She gave him a dirty look. You don't get it, she'd said. You never listen. You don't understand it at all.

After they separated, she sometimes called in the middle of the night. I could hear him whispering to her and pictured him, just a room away, huddled in the bathroom telling her to grow up, to be an adult, to call someone else, he wasn't her lifeline anymore. But he always went. He'd put on his clothes and kiss my forehead because he was worried about what she might do to herself, and in the end his concern for her safety trumped his deep feelings of righteous antagonism for the years of his life he'd dedicated to this needful, rageful woman.

I'd lie in bed and imagine what he was saying to her, how he'd pry sleeping pills, Advil bottles, a razor, whatever out of her hands and talk to her like she was a child, someone who was no longer a threat but something to fix, to put to bed, to pet the hair of until it went to sleep. He would come back to me as dawn was breaking, creep in so

Raha Raissnia, *Galvanoscope 1*, 2018. Projector, 16mm film, wood, scrim. 3 min. loop. Sculpture dimensions: 23 x 31 x 31 inches. Overall installation dimensions variable. Edition of 2 + 1 AP. Courtesy of the artist and Miguel Abreu Gallery, New York. Photo: Stephen Faught

as not to wake me, and take a shower to reset himself, start fresh, before slipping into bed. The daylight washed away whatever psychotic energy she'd been harboring in the darkness and she would leave him, us, alone for a while. Those nights when he had gone to her, when I was imagining them together, I was very trusting, hardly jealous. I was proud of him for protecting us; imagine the guilt, however unfounded, he would harbor, I'd think, were she to die — the way it would knot him up inside, twist him, rend his loving heart in two. Of course, that's exactly what happened.

❧

There were no blinds on any of the windows in the rooms, and a skylight poured light right onto the bed, so although he hadn't slept well the night before — when he did get to sleep he'd had a series of disturbing, murky dreams that evaporated when the sunlight hit — he woke up early, just after 6:00 a.m. The day stretched out before him. So many empty days. He was there for two weeks. He and his girlfriend had decided not to call each other while he was there, but he missed her reassuring voice. He dug his phone out of the dresser and dialed. She didn't pick up, and he didn't leave a message. He didn't feel nervous, exactly — it was Monday, she was at work; no, it was 6:07 a.m., she was asleep — but he did feel unsettled. A walk would help. Fresh air.

Maybe he'd sign up for one of the weirdo pseudoscience brain things; they were expensive, but artists at the Center were entitled to one free session. It was unlikely that the scan itself would significantly improve his creative prowess in regard to the particular nonstory he was working on at the moment — three overworked paragraphs on the mindset of an indeterminate narrator did not a novel make — but maybe just interacting with strangers would help unlock something. And anyway, he'd quite like a picture of his brain to frame for his living room. What a talking piece.

The signup board was on the wall in the dining room, which was empty except for a woman, late 60s, with long gray hair, who was sitting at a table gazing into space. He scanned the list of programs, some, like the sweat lodge sessions, held weekly, some monthly, some longer day- and week-long courses. There was a vaguely Judeo-Christian tone to them — Light-building workshops and Triad Location.

He sometimes wished he had faith. In sin, in absolving, in a higher power. One afternoon while his girlfriend went for a run in the park, he'd trekked up to St. John the Divine and sat down in the dark cavernous space, hoping to feel something. But the service was in English instead of in Latin, as he'd expected, and a woman with a reedy voice sang an annoying, monotone song that referred with jarring regularity to Jesus Christ Our Lord, whom Henry didn't believe in.

He put his name down for a scan the following day and walked back out into the heat. He would burn. Maybe his girlfriend had packed him sunscreen. He felt something behind him and turned to find the woman had followed him outside.

"We know her here," she said, pleased. "Has she come back too?"

"Sorry, who's this?"

"I thought it was you. We've been waiting to meet you."

Henry regarded the woman as one would a small wild creature. Something not inherently dangerous, but unpredictable and unlikely. A racoon out in the middle of the day. He said, as if in a movie, "I think you've mistaken me for someone else."

"Let her know she should come back. I've felt her energy; it wants to be here. She was very close to a breakthrough. She'll get there if she does the work."

"I certainly have to do the work," he said, cheerfully. "Back at it indeed. I'll head there now." He walked past her, back to the barn. From the window in the bedroom he watched her stand there for a long time until, suddenly, she turned and stalked through the long grasses and into the trees.

He wrote. He went to dinner. He slept. In the morning he made his way through the early heat to yet another nondescript wooden building for his scan, and when he got inside it looked nothing like he'd imagined, which was somehow a combination of Brooklyn new age, cream and gold, and a dingy doctor's office. It was just a large clean room divided down the middle by glass or some thick plastic, like an airplane window, and on the other side of that clear wall was a large machine. The scanner, he assumed. It was quiet, cool.

Two people were there to greet him, Dr. Meyerson and Ray, both professional -looking sixtysomethings, and after a moment of confusion Henry realized that Ray looked so familiar because she was the strange woman who'd followed him about yesterday babbling about Lily, or not Lily, something he didn't understand. What was that? She made no gesture of recognition now. In something of a daze, he let them greet him and explain the procedure. Dr. Meyerson injected something — you may feel a warm sensation, something like urination as this sets in, but don't worry, it's not happening, he said — and they talked about his life like he was answering a deposition. He was unfeeling when he mentioned Lily's death, and if either of them knew who Lily was they didn't make a sign. He talked about writing, how he'd had trouble for the last year or so, how his girlfriend had found a pamphlet on the Center and suggested he come up though he wasn't sure about all this extra stuff, ha ha, he just needed time and space to think, and then they had him climb onto a table that slid him into the big scanning machine and he couldn't tell if they were in the room anymore, though Ray's voice came, soothingly, through some speaker inside the bright close chamber. She started making various statements, basically repeating things to him that he had already said, as well as adding some standard psychoanalytic BS about childhood, about parents, *I feel proud of my accomplishments*, *I am in love with my current partner*, et cetera, et cetera, until he was nearly asleep.

After a while Ray said, "We're going to bring you back out," and the lights shut off in the machine and he slid out into the room.

"Come," Dr. Meyerson said, "Sit. How are you feeling. Here, have some water. Shall we go through? Ray and I are going to use phrases like 'light up' and 'fire' to describe the brain imagery. If you are uncomfortable with these words, please let me know and we can adjust the terminology."

"Um, no, that's fine." Ray was sitting serenely next to her husband, clicking around on the computer in front of her and making no sign that she remembered their previous meeting. He couldn't see the screen, for all he knew it was blank, but they peered at it together and started to say things like frontolimbic network and right superior anterior temporal lobe and subgenual cingulate cortex and sadness and blockage and depression and possibility and kinetic and guilt and guilt and guilt, and did he feel guilty? Were there feelings of guilt? Was the guilt what was stopping him from working? And finally, he said, Thank you, no offense, this just wasn't for him, and walked out through the field and toward the woods but not into them, it looked so cool in there but there was no clear trail, there were maybe ticks. He was thinking about the letter Lily had written to his girlfriend a few weeks before she died. He'd been in his girlfriend's apartment one evening and she had just run out to buy some eggs, and then he heard footsteps outside the apartment door and then there was an envelope pushed under it. When he opened the door whoever it was had gone, and he knew it was Lily so he opened the letter. And then he kept the letter and eventually put it in his bedside table and forgot about it, and months after Lily died in the car accident, when his girlfriend was looking for some stamps, she found it and brought it to him looking horrified. Oh, god, he said, I should have told you about this, she wrote it when things were so dark and I found it and — It's true we got in knock-down, drag-out fights — I've told you about the way she'd stand in front of me, goading me to hit her, telling me about everything she'd done, the men, the lies, it was — it was unbearable. I did shove her once, something that will haunt me. But the things she was saying, I couldn't take it, the taunting, and I pushed her away from me. She stumbled and fell against the couch. I've never been so disgusted at myself. But that's all, my love, that is the worst of it. You know me. You know I would never hurt her or you or anyone. Oh, love, you're bleeding. What have you done to your little paw? He took my pointer finger, which I'd been picking at, and held it up, the nail red and wet with blood, and opened his mouth and put it in. I could feel the warmth of his tongue, the soft slick of his lips, the gentlest scrape from his teeth as he pulled my finger out and held it up to me, clean. "There," he said. "Like new."

I've tried to convince myself that humans are not particles, that I can't be entangled with Henry, or his dead wife, or anyone else in the universe, but it's a hard notion to shake. And when Henry is away, to my mind, he is in two states at once. He has not been confirmed as alive or dead, and so he is either and both. And it's more than two states. Ten thousand states. He is in the shower and in bed and kissing a stranger and weeping alone and eating his dinner and shooting himself in the head. He is writing and not writing and breathing and not breathing.

I would not call myself a creative person, not exactly — I cannot make a story out of nothing — but when given a tangle of words, I can see the central threads and tug them out. It's what makes me so well suited to my job. Given time and space to sit with a story, I can figure out where it's going, and where it should go, and when it should end in hope and when it should end in mourning and when, sometimes, there can be both.

When Henry called, so early in the morning, I was sitting at my kitchen table reading a manuscript. I had woken before dawn, and now the sun streaked the sky outside lavender. I listened to his call come in and then I let it ring itself out.

Back at the barn he took a pull from the whiskey he'd brought, just in case. He felt settled, like dropping into a hot bath. He wrote. He drank a little more. He went to dinner, needing human contact, and sat down near a trio that looked mostly normal and they started talking to him, happy to engage in a positive exchange of ideas. He told them he'd come here because his girlfriend had told him to, because she was really into the woo-woo astrology stuff, the meditation, the occult, though that wasn't true, it was Lily who'd been into that, his girlfriend had shown none of those proclivities thank god, but what did it matter to these strangers. You're just like Yeats, one of them said, and they all laughed. Henry laughed too but he didn't get it. When he got back to his room he turned the internet back on so he could find out what they'd found so funny, and learned that Yeats dabbled in mysticism, bouncing through women who were engaged in practices of automatic writing and psychic reading and aura work. For his whole life he was in love with one woman who didn't want him. He proposed five times and she said no every time and the last time, after he'd finished crying, he went and proposed to her daughter, who also said no. He got married a couple weeks later to another woman, the automatic writer, and then he had one trillion affairs including with a famous lesbian and then he died and his wife and the first love both came to his deathbed so all that suffering seemed a little performative, in the end, since he got more or less exactly what he wanted. He didn't want to be happy with the first love, not really — he got too much material from the angst. So much poetry from so much suffering. He'd probably liked it, the sadness.

Maybe that was what Lily was. Maybe it was best that she died when she did because now she was perfect and contained, and maybe this was the point — maybe he needed to write about *her* and maybe that's why he'd been blocked. It wasn't guilt, it wasn't spiritual, it was the memory of her, the alive memory that needed to come out. When they were together, she used to tell him not to put her in a novel, and he hadn't. And even when he left her, when she'd call in the night and he'd return to her like she was a drug, she'd still be weepy and irritating, and why couldn't she just be easy, ever? — even then he didn't write about her, he honored that request. Sometimes he did give her Ambien when she asked for her migraine pills, he'd even dumped some into the same bottle. They looked nothing alike of course, but he'd seen the way she scrabbled in the dark for her pills, the way she threw them back without looking at them. It was not malicious. He didn't quite know why he did it. He'd started doing it around the time he went through her desk and found the novel he hadn't known she was writing. Fiction was his. A few weeks later he started talking to the pretty assistant in his editor's office. So the pills were some power thing, maybe, if he was going to psychoanalyze. When they did the autopsy after the accident and found the sleeping pills in her system there was nothing to suspect that he had anything to do with it — and he didn't. Maybe she'd taken the sleeping pills on purpose. She was so troubled. If it hadn't been the car it would have been something else. And what right had she to be driving?

Henry was writing, now, writing out his rage, writing his wife out of him. He'd abandoned his laptop, it was too distancing, why had anyone decided that computers were a good idea, the hand needed the pen, the pen needed the paper — and in fact he wasn't writing at all, he was exorcising, he was confessing — but there was nothing to confess! He had done nothing wrong! That woman, whispering weird things at him, that idiotic scan — was it possible that Lily had been here? Was that why she'd told him to come? No, it was his girlfriend who'd found the place, he kept reminding himself, not Lily. They were two separate humans, unconnected. If Lily had come here, his girlfriend wouldn't have known. Unless she'd found the pamphlet in one of the old books, tucked away, some bit he hadn't found himself. There was a distant ringing, an alarm somewhere. Was it his? No. The phone was off, dead, dark. Perhaps his girlfriend had sent him away in order to be alone with his things. She had days and days to discover. Would she go poking about? When she'd found that letter Lily wrote to her, with all those terrible accusations, awful things about his character, about his rage — why hadn't he gotten rid of that letter when he'd found it poked under their door? Why had he secreted it away like that? Hoarding it. Unwilling to let it go. It had been so strange to see the worst parts of himself laid out, like that, on the page. It was one-sided. But were parts of it true? Was that really him? It had taken a day of remonstration, of assurance, of reminders that Lily had been crazy, not in her right mind, desperate to drive them apart. He'd stopped his night-time visits to Lily after finding that letter. It was hard to stay away; though he hated her she had also become more attractive to him when he had his girlfriend at home, too. But the letter had been too far, she'd gone too far with that. So he stopped going to her when she called, and then two weeks later she was dead. But why hadn't he disposed of that letter. Now, like a sheepdog with a taste for blood, his girlfriend would be on the hunt for other clues. Would she get into the back of that bottom drawer? Why had he held onto her manuscript? She would find it, know he'd hidden it, and that was as bad as murder, or it would be to her. Keeping her work from its would-be readers. She would find the nearly finished novel, the poetry, which he kept in his desk, so easy to find — why had he left it so easy to find, because of course she had been so trustful, so loyal, so unlike Lily there was no reason to hide anything. She would find them, and she was a good reader, she would see how good they were. Oh god, he could picture her taking them to her editor at work, showing them to him in awe. She was ambitious, gently so, but ambitious. She cared about the work, she would think she was doing god's work, bringing Lily back, discovering her — what did Lily care if she was discovered, she was dead wasn't she? But now his young, sweet girlfriend, all quiet ambition, would find her words, all those words. She'd think he was the monster who had silenced her. She had been so difficult. He had loved her. He had tried. That ringing. A fire alarm somewhere. Not in the house, no, perhaps in one of the main buildings. He couldn't write anymore, his thoughts had returned, he was all thought now, so much useless thought. And it was too hot up there in the barn. From the window he could see something glowing through the trees, and perhaps that's where the ringing was coming from, from the trees, somehow, or from the electric beyond. Outside it was cool and dark, and the further he got from the barn, the closer to the woods, the darker it got although, above, the sky was incandescent with stars. Darkness, deeper darkness, something both dark and burning — he walked toward it.

POEM DREAMT ON A PLANE, OR, FRAGILITY

JAVIER ZAMORA

There was a mouse. I didn't have eyes.
I was sitting in an aisle seat, got up, blocked the passageway,
told passengers: ¡there's a mouse in this plane!
Not even the mouse cared —
she lived in this plane.
She approached, her whiskers sensing thunderstorms.
I sat there, waiting. Then, I woke.
Got my computer out, began writing
there was a mouse, changed the font from Times
to Garamond. Sensing —

years after she walked into the Washington Square Park
fountain with all her clothes on in late October,
drunk from red wine she'd downed at the dinner
I told her I'd stopped loving her,
perhaps never loved her, she cried
so much her eyes puffed up like she didn't have eyes,
& I didn't do, or say, anything —

there's a chance she'll read this.
G,
I'm trying to return my fragility
but I don't have a receipt. I was oblivious
to apologizing — I'd misunderstood.
You are not a cashier. I should never
have said "you're crazy," "jealous," "stupid,"
"calm down," drank so much. Somehow
I end up pointing at my father, uncles,
grandfathers, but it's me who opened my mouth.
I'm sorry.

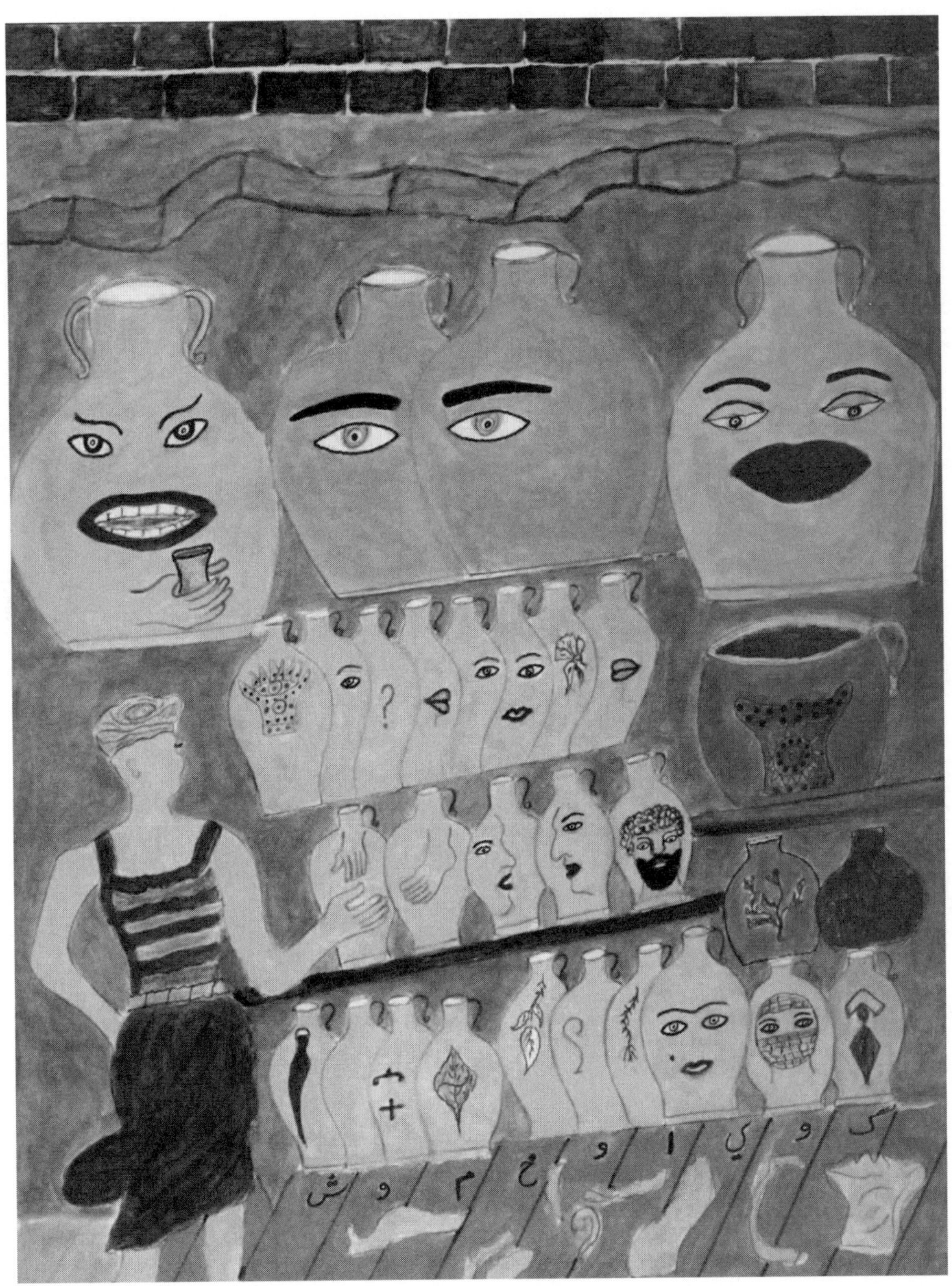

Reza Shafahi, *Gooya Khamoosh,* 2014, Acrylic, oil & Marker on paper, 50 x 70 cm. Courtesy of the artist

Reza Shafahi, *World Viewer Cow*, 2018. Acrylic, oil & marker on paper. 50 x 35 cm. Courtesy of the artist

LA GLOBALIZATION MUCH GOOD VERY WEALTH

JAVIER ZAMORA

having discovered otters hold hands while sleeping   que cute   much adorable
    the Government needed a research question to grasp the "Free Market"
Scientists asked much money to answer   pero guai *do* otters hold hands

    Neo-Liberals passed budget-cuts   Socialists picketed to save the much sad
mangrove forests   thousands fled north   hundreds south   the president
    demanded many kelp   many urchins   sending much love to otters
from president who was cousins with two senators   many fortunes

    you're very good primos   one told the other   we much concerned
with environment   we buy less threatening   less curious animal to our waters
    much applause   much approval rating more high for president

a market bump after bill signed   #muchmoney   #parade   many floats
    many people half naked not working   confetti balloons
much trash   many trampled   news retweet trending   much sad   very bad

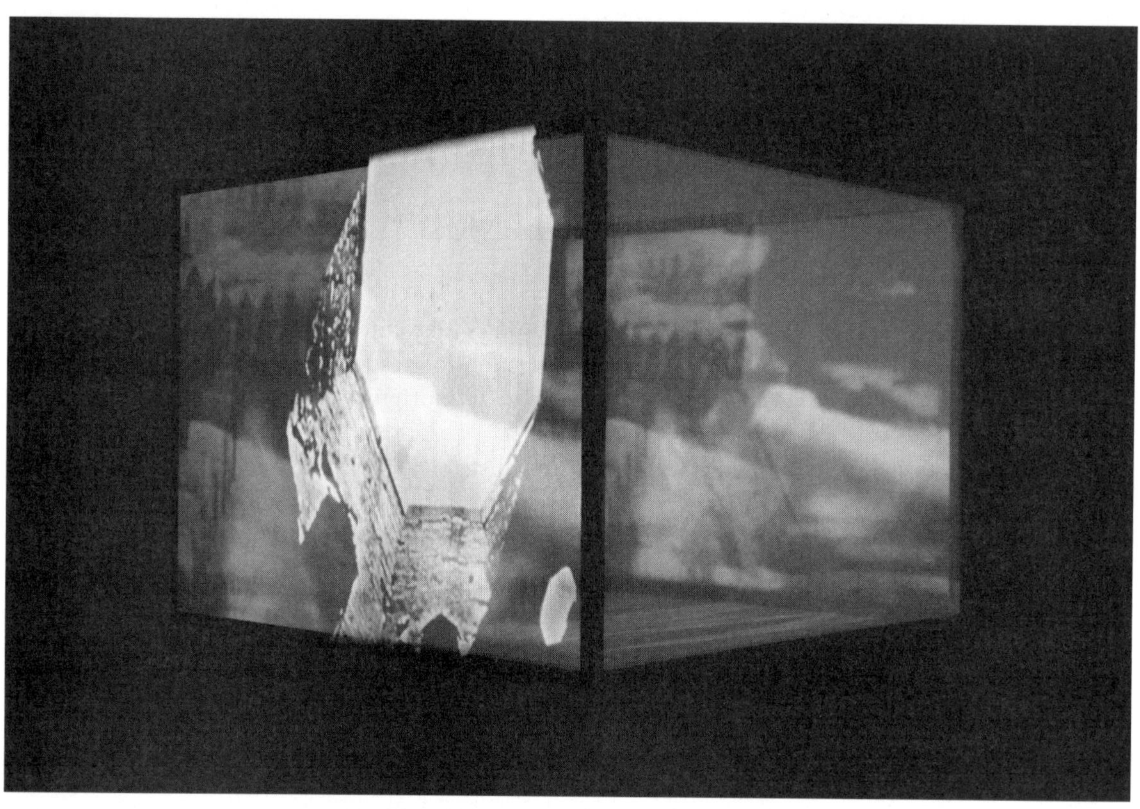

Raha Raissnia, *Galvanoscope 2 (Film A and film B)*, 2018. Two projectors, two 16mm films, wood, scrim. 3 min. loop. Sculpture dimensions: 23 3/8 x 32 x 32 inches. Overall installation dimensions variable. Edition of 2 + 1 AP. Courtesy of the artist and Miguel Abreu Gallery, New York. Photo: Stephen Faught

CELERY JUICE & SKINNED FROGS: A BRIEF HISTORY OF MEDICAL MEDIUMS

ADAM MORRIS

Due to the laxity of laws regulating the sale of medicine in 19th-century America, itinerant peddlers traveled nationwide, selling miracle remedies for every sort of ailment. These salesmen seldom claimed insight to the secret recipes for the tinctures, powders, and tonics they sold, attributing them instead to mysterious doctors operating in faraway cities, or to healers residing in distant lands.

Contemporary snake-oil salesmen haven't cast aside this ruse. They've merely updated the methods for capitalizing on the credulity of their marks: after cherry-picking findings from the dietary studies published in science journals each year, health faddists take to social media, where they trade upon their own celebrity as bloggers, television personalities, and Instagram influencers to hawk dietary regimens, nutritional supplements, anti-aging treatments, and routines for general "wellness."

New York Times best-selling author Anthony William is a notable exception to this pattern. William calls himself the "originator of the Global Celery Juice Movement," a dietary trend whose practitioners drink a large quantity of fresh celery juice on an empty stomach each morning. (He recommends a daily dose of 16 ounces, the amount produced by juicing one large bunch of celery.) William claims that millions of people around the world now practice this bracing matinal routine, and that it has healed countless suffers of sundry ailments, including allergies, eczema, psoriasis, migraines, high blood pressure, acid reflux, and gout. On his website, William lists praise from Sylvester Stallone, Pharrell Williams, Robert De Niro, and other Hollywood celebrities who have relied on his advice.

But Anthony William is not a doctor. He is neither a nutritionist, nor a scientist, nor even the sort of practitioner credentialed with the mysterious acronyms dispensed by alternative medicine degree mills. Although he describes himself as a "man of science," William professes to have no use for clinical trials or research studies: his medical wisdom does not flow from a source as crass as a peer-reviewed journal.

That is because Anthony William is a spirit medium; he obtains his knowledge of the human body, its various maladies, and their surprising cures from the Beyond. As William succinctly states on his website, he "was born with the unique ability to converse with [a] Spirit of Compassion who provides him with extraordinarily accurate health information that's often far ahead of its time." This Spirit, he has made clear, doesn't belong to a specific departed human soul, like those one might encounter during a séance in Lily Dale. Instead, "Spirit" is William's shorthand for a supra-individual, quasi-transcendental collective compassion — with compassion conceived as wisdom rather than as sentiment.

William has communed with the Spirit since 1975, when he was four years old. That year, the toddler "shocked his family" by announcing that his grandmother had lung cancer. This was surprising news to everyone, including the afflicted woman. (She felt fine.) Conventional doctors later arrived at the same diagnosis, but William did not require their tests or validation: the Spirit had insisted it was so.

Following this momentous prediction, William continued to develop his gift for clairaudient diagnosis, with the assistance of his familiar Spirit. This led in due course to his lucrative career as the so-called "Medical Medium." For a fee, William identifies previously undiagnosed ailments and offers restorative prescriptions for patients suffering symptoms with unknown causes. He considers himself the most recent exponent of the lineage of "savants who know things that computers have difficulty coming up with": a long line of healers and seers who have emerged throughout human history "from time immemorial."

William believes most of his patients suffer from a range of autoimmune diseases that can be remedied by dietary means. According to the Spirit of Compassion, the ill effects of inflammation, acidity, and environmental toxins can be cured by things like pears and freshly squeezed juices. In his practice, as well as in his books and videos, William relays this advice to his clients. Because the Spirit apparently regards celery juice as a panacea for an endless array of ailments, the Global Celery Juice Movement emerged from these prescriptions.

In his capacity as a medical medium, William is merely the latest exponent of a long tradition in psychic healing. Writing about the Global Celery Juice Movement for *The Baffler*, Kristen Martin observes that William has publicly compared himself to Edgar Cayce, a clairvoyant healer who conducted thousands of psychic diagnoses in the early 20th century. Known as the "sleeping prophet," Cayce toured the United States to promulgate his teachings on aura-reading, the Dead Sea Scrolls, reincarnation, and additional subjects of interest to early 20th-century occult enthusiasts and mystics. Cayce was deeply influenced by the writings of the occultist Helena Petrovna Blavatsky, as well as other writers associated with her Theosophical Society; he claimed his teachings derived from the "Akashic records." Known alternately as the "Book of Life," the Akashic records are a cosmic archive of universal knowledge and a repository of the wisdom and experiences of everyone who has ever lived — all of it etched, somehow, into the cosmic ether. Cayce possessed a clairvoyant power that enabled him to "read" the Akashic records while immersed in a hypnotic trance. Duly recorded by his secretary Gladys, Cayce's trance dictations became the basis of his prolific output of published works, which are still issued by the organization that guards his legacy, the Association for Research and Enlightenment. American religious historians generally acknowledge Edgar Cayce to be the principal fountainhead of what became known as "New Age" thought: a vast and shapeless genre of anti-rationalist Western esotericism which draws deeply on Eastern religions and mysticism.

But Cayce was far from original. Just as William had partly fashioned himself on Cayce, the latter was inspired by a celebrity healer who gained fame and adoration a century prior. Although nearly forgotten by the time Cayce embarked on his career as a psychic and teacher, a clairvoyant healer named Andrew Jackson Davis was one of the most notorious celebrities of antebellum America.

Davis was born in 1826 in Blooming Grove, New York, to an illiterate mother and a booze-addled cobbler. According to his colorfully embellished autobiography, an inebriated villager known as Uncle Thomas was permitted to name the child when he was four days old, his parents having to neglected to christen their sixth child and second son. The tipsy farmer named the future seer after Old Hickory, the national war hero and soon-to-be American president.

Clairvoyance was said to run in the Davis family. Believing her to be psychic, neighbors consulted Mrs. Davis whenever livestock or farm equipment went missing. Mother and son both experienced sleepwalking visions, which Mrs. Davis would interpret according to folk superstitions. After Mrs. Davis's death and the rapid failure of her husband's attempts to run a general store, young Jackson left home to apprentice with a Poughkeepsie boot and shoe salesman. It was about this time, in 1843, that the city of Poughkeepsie was entranced by the "mesmeric miracles" performed by a visiting lecturer called Dr. Stanley Grimes, who had already become famous on the athenaeum lecture circuit for his awe-inspiring phrenological readings.

Mesmerism was a belated American import of European provenance and 18th-century vintage. The discipline was named for Franz Anton Mesmer (1734–1815), a German doctor practicing in Vienna. Titled *The Influence of the Planets on the Human Body*

(1765), Mesmer's dissertation bore one of the hallmarks of Western occultism: the law of cosmic correspondences. Mesmer hypothesized a direct correspondence between planetary alignments and human health. Celestial movements, he theorized, altered forces of "universal gravitation" already operating between smaller bodies on planets such as Earth. At the microcosmic level of the human body, Mesmer called this force "animal magnetism." By 1774, Mesmer had begun to experiment with ways of influencing animal magnetism, including the application of magnets to various parts of the human body, sonic baths of music produced on a glass harmonica, and a primitive form of hypnotism that would soon bear his name.

Austrian authorities disapproved of Mesmer's occult theories. Hoping to practice in the capital of Enlightenment science, the doctor decamped to Paris, only to be roundly discredited by a committee of scientists convened by Louis XVI to evaluate the worth of his teachings. (Benjamin Franklin was one of the committee's illustrious members.) Although Mesmer was ridiculed by his peers, not all of his students found the damning royal report sufficient reason to suspend their studies of animal magnetism. Most prominent among those who advanced the occult science was the Marquis de Puységur, who hypothesized that a state of somnambulant clairvoyance might be induced in certain predisposed subjects. This half-sleep state became known as mesmeric trance and would soon be a standard part of a medical practice already disavowed by its namesake.

Mesmer wanted nothing to do with the somnambulant school of medicine, which allowed entranced clairvoyants to diagnose maladies by gazing into the interior of the human body. The practice flourished anyway, and was later carried to American shores by Charles Poyen, a French physician who became a convert to mesmeric healing after a clairvoyant precisely described the symptoms of a painful digestive condition he suffered. While attempting to convalesce on a relative's colonial sugar plantation, Poyen practiced mesmerizing some of the family's black servants (perhaps slaves) before ultimately departing for New England, where he ingratiated himself among anti-slavery activists by publishing abolitionist tracts.

Poyen was surprised to discover that mesmeric science was practically unknown in Massachusetts when he arrived. Discerning an opportunity, he launched a lecture series at Boston's Chauncey Hall in January 1836. After his lessons were met with skepticism and indifference, Poyen realized that Americans could not be persuaded by intricate theories; they would only be convinced by demonstrations. Eventually he found a magnetic subject ideal for providing such proofs. This was Cynthia Ann Gleason, a longtime sufferer of digestive and sleeping disorders that Poyen managed to cure. Gleason agreed to act as Poyen's subject in public demonstrations at Brown University and Harvard Medical School. After placing her into a mesmeric trance, Poyen used magnets to move Gleason's limbs while she remained otherwise unresponsive, then proceeded to have her clairvoyantly diagnose the ailments of various audience members. Relative success in these august academic venues was checked by criticism from the Boston press. Undeterred, Poyen and Gleason hit the road to lecture in smaller towns throughout New

England. Their demonstrations regularly included the recruitment of volunteers from among the spectators, whose subsequent entrancement titillated villagers throughout New England.

One disciple of Poyen's evangelism was Stanley Grimes, whose work on behalf of the new science had placed him on stage before the young Andrew Jackson Davis. At Grimes's Poughkeepsie lecture, Davis was one of those who wished to "test the matter by personal trial" and experience the "mysterious slumber" cast by the mesmerist. But Grimes was unable to magnetize him, in spite of Davis's predisposition to sleepwalking. After Grimes left town, a tailor by the name of William Livingstone felt it was time for a career change, and decided to try his hand at mesmeric operation. Jackson agreed to sit for another test, and was easily magnetized on Livingstone's first attempt. While Jackson remained submerged in a somnambulant trance, Livingstone sent for an audience to witness the boy's mesmeric feats, which included reading a newspaper while blindfolded.

Jackson's ability to see "through the forehead" made him a local celebrity, and marked the beginning of a long and profitable engagement between Livingstone and his talented assistant. As Jackson sharpened his skills, he ascended into higher magnetic "states" in which he experienced enhanced powers of clairvoyance. In the third such state, Jackson could see the magnetic aura, or "light atmosphere" that surrounded each human form. Meanwhile, bodies became as transparent as glass, allowing Jackson to perceive their glowing guts, with each organ expressing a different luminescent quality.

In 1844, after conducting an exhausting demonstration in a private home, Jackson accidentally fell back into the mesmeric state and found his consciousness projected on to a mountaintop graveyard in the Catskills, where he communed with the spirits of two of his forebears in occult science. The first of these was the Greek physician Galen, who gave Jackson a spring-loaded walking stick that contained lists of all the diseases that afflict mankind, as well as occult recipes for their cures. This was the cane referenced in the title of Davis's autobiography, *The Magic Staff.* The second spirit revealed that Davis was destined to be the prophet who would transmit higher knowledge from the spiritual world to the terrestrial sphere: "By thee will a new light appear," the spirit told him, "and it will establish that which has been, and still is supposed to be the wildest hallucination, *viz.*, the law and 'kingdom of heaven' on earth." This magnificent decree was uttered by the spirit of the 18th-century Swedish mystic Emanuel Swedenborg, who promised to watch over Davis as he expounded to the masses, warning that the wisdom Davis revealed would "surprise and confound those of the land who are considered deeply versed in science and metaphysics."

After these grand pronouncements, Jackson found it difficult to return to performing for "large-eyed and open-mouthed seekers for signs and wonders." They only wanted him to read the hour from a pocket-watch while wearing a blindfold, gaze serenely into their bellies to identify the contents of their dinners, or describe the interiors of faraway homes. But Jackson resolved to dispense with such frivolous demonstrations to attend to those truly in need of his services: the sick. The curative recommendations that Jackson received from Galen were often much more eccentric than celery juice: Jackson once instructed a man to cure his oncoming deafness by draping the warm skins of freshly killed rats over his ears. Another man, seeking relief from an abscess that threatened the loss of his finger, was told to bind the corpse of skinned frog to the afflicted flesh.

With Jackson's talents and Livingstone's skilled management, the two earned double Livingstone's previous salary. But Jackson harbored doubts about Livingstone's abilities as a mesmeric operator, and suspected his clairvoyant development was being restrained by Livingstone's limits. The tailor soon perceived his subject's restlessness and accused him of eyeing other operators. He was right to be concerned: after a trance vision convinced Jackson that the time for separation had arrived, he ran off to Connecticut to begin work with a new operator, a botanist and clergyman named Silas Smith Lyon. The latter hastily sold his botanical medical practice, furnishing the funds required for the pair to establish themselves in New York City, where they settled in November 1845.

In New York, Andrew Jackson Davis became a celebrity of unusual proportions. While still a teenager, Jackson began delivering clairvoyant lectures while entranced in the "superior state." These occasions attracted some of the city's intellectual elite to the duo's Vesey Street boardinghouse, many of them taken in by Jackson's muddled paraphrases of Swedenborgian theology, which was then in vogue among the city's progressive clergy. Reports of Jackson's powers traveled by word of mouth until Horace Greeley's *New York Tribune* transcribed some of the "remarkable phenomena" Lyon had elicited from his subject. Among the curious investigators drawn to Jackson's trance lectures was the popular socialist and *Tribune* columnist, Albert Brisbane. Another visitor was a man with "feminine mental characteristics" and a brain whose aura shined with dazzling luminescence. This was Edgar Allan Poe. Like Ben Franklin before him, Poe was skeptical of mesmerism, referring to it as one of the "matters which put to the severest test the credulity or, more precisely, the faith of mankind." But although mesmeric medicine had its fair share of detractors, the practice continued to thrive among antebellum progressives attracted to the other popular fads of the 1840s, including dress reform, water-cure, homeopathy, Grahamism, and women's suffrage. When Jackson's trance-lectures were published in 1847 as *The Principles of Nature, Her Divine Revelations: A Message to Mankind*, the book became the 19th-century equivalent of a best seller, and garnered an unprecedented amount of prepublication publicity.

Lyon and Jackson continued to sustain themselves on medical consultations. Many of these were conducted in person, but other patients, too sick to travel or residing far from New York City, sent locks of hair and descriptions of their symptoms, with the hopes of receiving a long-distance diagnosis by post. Jackson incautiously advertised this ability, which occasionally brought trouble: he found himself the center of ridicule when a healthy priest, acting to defend Christianity against the new heathen science, wrote pretending to be a sick woman and received, in response, a syrup prescribed for the tuberculosis that Jackson diagnosed by stroking the lock of blond hair the priest had enclosed in his letter.

Mesmeric medicine was eventually banned in New York, largely due to pressures from the newly founded school of "eclectic" medicine, which included homeopathy, herbal medicine, and electric therapy. But the belief system undergirding mesmeric clairvoyance apparently remains in place more than a century later. Anthony William continues to amass followers, no matter his dubious methods. Today is April 14, 2019, and according to Google, the words "celery juice" were published online more than 20,000 times in the past 24 hours.

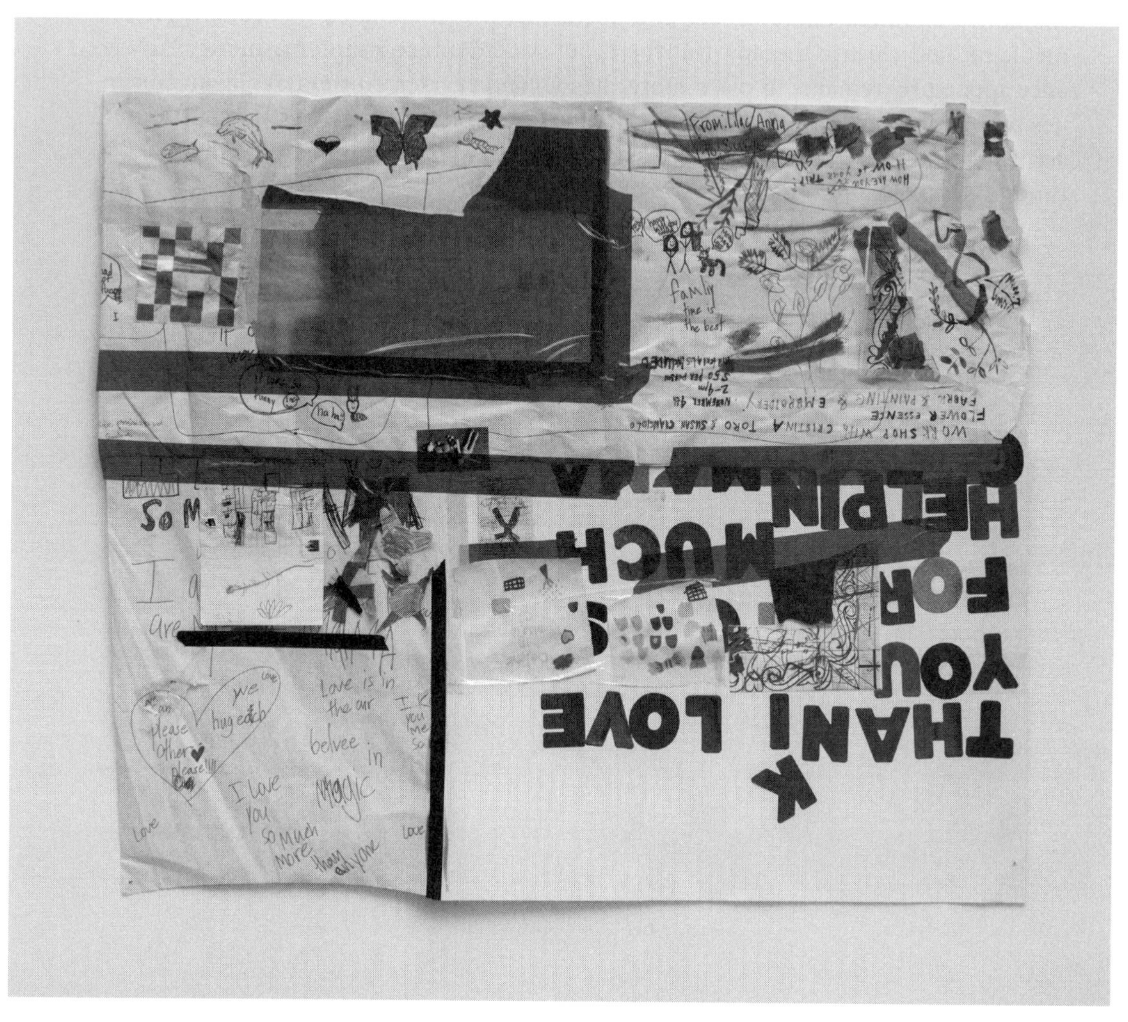

Susan Cianciolo, *Thank You For Helping Collage*, 2016-2017. Stickers, marker, tape, pen, water-based paint, collage on paper, 44 ½ × 37 ¼ inches. Image courtesy of the Overduin & Co., Los Angeles

MOTHER OF CUPS

ZOE TUCK

Have you seen *Buffy*? Her mom's name is Joyce Summers. She's kind of a fringe character for most of the series. That's part of what feels exciting about the show — the main characters, still in high school when the series begins, seem somewhat free to navigate the world on their own terms. There are teachers and principals, but mostly there is fighting evil and learning how to
be a person.
Joyce is usually portrayed as terminally clueless. To be fair, most of the populace seems equally clueless and possessed of an almost infinite capacity to rationalize or forget
being attacked
again and again
having their loved ones dragged to a screaming death or seeing them return, but evil.
Finally (and here I am making assumptions about Buffy's writers), Joyce's cluelessness becomes too ridiculous, even for a show that walks the line between gravitas and farce, or perhaps it was that the writers of a show targeted at young adults starring young adults wanted
to address
topical issues
like coming out to your parents.
Except that — and this is what interests me as a trans woman — the series already depicts the coming of age/coming out story of a lesbian. So, why the need to have two coming out stories,
that is, Willow's and Buffy's?

There are three likely possibilities.
Buffy's coming out narrative precedes Willow's, so perhaps it was a way to test the waters with
a coded reference to queer sexuality. That's option one.
What if both stories were planned in advance? In that case, it's possible that Buffy's coming out story was a well-meaning (if perhaps inaccurate) attempt on behalf of the show's writers to say, "Hey, everyone has secrets or plans or attributes that diverge from those of their mothers?
We're all kind of alike, aren't we?"
The last option and, I believe, the least likely, is that the writers wanted to leave room for another way of being queer, whether that is a coded expression of an actually existing kind of sexual or gender difference (hey!) or a more mystical expression of a difference which could
exist, but does not yet exist, borne back to us from the threshold of the possible.
But what does this have to do with mothers?
Tonight I watched season three, episode 11, "Gingerbread." At this point in the series, Joyce has discovered that her daughter is The Slayer and asked, "Have you tried not being a slayer?" By this point she has reconciled herself somewhat to Buffy's slaying, going so far as to accompany her on her nightly patrol of Sunnydale's vast, high-traffic graveyards.
Joyce finds two dead children, and her horror causes her to lead the town in a literal crusade against witchcraft which begins with a town meeting, whose theme is "Never Again," organized by Joyce, but introduced by the town's secretly evil mayor. It ends with Buffy, Willow, and Amy tied to stakes above burning pyres which their own families and neighbors have lit. There is a happy ending of sorts, orchestrated from the margins by Giles, the librarian, and Cordelia, a member of the slayer's "Scooby Gang." The townsfolk, it seems, were possessed by an evil spirit, posing as two small children, who goaded them to ever more extreme acts of destruction because of
little ghosts who say
i'm still scared of the bad girls
you have to make them go away
Cordelia douses the flames, Giles incants a spell causing the spirit to reveal its true form, Buffy stakes it.
But why is it so easy for Joyce, and the other parents (although I must stress that the emphasis is on moms), to hate all witches because of the (supposed) actions of a few? Why was she unable to see the good witches for the bad?

Why, for that matter, are witches, more than non-witches, spoken and thought of in these binaristic terms?
It is as if she had already prepared a place in her heart for hate or had a place prepared for her.
Why does the real work of fighting evil in Sunnydale happen on the fringe, while it is so comparatively easy for a bewitched PTA to work with the official mechanisms of power
the school administration
the police
the mayor
This is what I mean by a place prepared for hate.
I think of Giles as Halperin's deviant teacher, within the system, but ever suspect, ever in danger
of being ejected from it.
I think of Laura Jane Klug, transgender teacher at Lumberton Texas ISD who was suspended
for no reason, except bigotry.
I think of my own mother, about whom I am grateful to confidently proclaim that she would never
lead a charge against me and others like me but who told me:
You know you're very suggestible
It's true
but implies
trans is catching
and that it's bad to catch
You're scared, mom, I hear that
but
Little ghost children are lying to you

Opposite: Ana Mendieta, *Árbol de la Vida (Tree of Life Series)*, 1976. Color photograph.

Above: Ana Mendieta, *Untitled: Silueta Series*, 1978. Still from super-8mm film transferred to high-definition digital media, color, silent. Running time: 3:14 minutes.

Reza Shafahi, *Untitled*, 2015. Acrylic, gouache & marker on paper. 70 x 51 cm. Courtesy of the artist

FEAR OF GOD

KRISTEN ARNETT

The three of us crowded together in the tiny hall bathroom and then we flipped off the light. We'd talked about it a little bit beforehand, but not much. Of course, we'd do it together, none of us alone in case *something* came for us. Safer in a group.

Why were we doing this?

Because we were 13 and because it was fun to feel scared.

One of the books we'd been secretly sharing included a scene at a sleepover where they'd done exactly this: entered a bathroom, turned off the light, and chanted the name "Bloody Mary" three times into a mirror. The anticipation of what you might find staring back you when you turned the light back on was heady stuff. Even talking about it made us scream a little. It was dangerous, calling on unseen forces. Those girls in the book hadn't gotten away from Mary, but we felt we had better odds.

In the dark, everything felt closer. Intimate. I discovered my own body by understanding how it felt in contrast to my friends. Here is my leg, touching that leg. Arms folding and unfolding, skin grazing. Fingers brushing. We huddled together and whispered "Bloody Mary" three times, per the ritual. We didn't know what the incantation might bring forth, but it seemed more exciting than anything else going on in our lives. Scary was better than nothing.

ഗ്ദ

We were girls who liked books, and what we liked most were the freaky ones that our evangelical parents refused to let us read. These were the pulp novels kept in grocery store checkout lines, sitting adjacent to the (also forbidden) romance novels. While the bodice rippers showcased breasts heaving with ecstasy, the horror novels had covers that featured the body dismembered: gnarled hands, faces in rictus, the pale-cheesy flesh of a bared thigh. Families hidden behind a second-page panel. Gothic family trees.

These books had vampires and werewolves and Ouija boards. There were monsters and murders. Haunted houses. Incest. Demons and ghosts. Serial killers. *Exorcisms.*

We read anything we could get our hands on: Stephen King, R. L. Stine, Christopher Pike, V. C. Andrews. Everything was kept hidden from our parents, shoved in the backs of closets and stuffed under mattresses. It was understood that those books belonged to the group and we'd only read them when we were together. We passed them around at sleepovers, whispering the worst bits in each other's ears. Those books told us about the afterlife and the infinite. They served as our new bibles.

These were midnight readings for the witching hour. We sat cross-legged on the floor and read aloud to each other, dog-earing the juicy parts for later discussion. The sex held allure, but it was because it was eroticism shrouded in fright. Anyone fucking in those books dealt with consequences much larger than pregnancy or disease. The horror-novel universe issued fornicators dire, otherworldly penalties. For girls who grew up Southern Baptist, this was a deeply familiar concept. Much like sex, the supernatural was something we were never supposed to discuss. According to our Sunday School teachers, even thinking about the paranormal could summon a devil. Dark matter. Things that couldn't be expelled from your brain or your heart.

It was exhilarating to read about these bodies housing hidden cravings, monstrous desires. The characters in these books were ravenous. They were hungry for everything forbidden. As a young lesbian who didn't yet know I was queer, I saw things about myself in those narratives. When we read those books together it was a shared experience with my friends, but it also felt deeply personal. Those characters worked so hard to fight off the demons that threatened to overtake them and were almost never successful. Whenever I looked at other girls in my life and wanted them, I felt haunted, too. I worked all day to expel those frightening, unwelcome thoughts. It was always a losing battle.

My friends and I often fell asleep discussing those books and their nightmare-inducing content. The suffering and terror of *My Sweet Audrina*. The ghoulish friendships of *Chain Letter 2*. The notion that according to *Pet Sematary*, sometimes dead is better. There were so many ways to hurt; so many ways to be scared. It was easy to find arousal in that fear, knowing that the things you often wanted the most were the things that could break you. How could a person be aware of their mortality without understanding that your life ultimately belonged to a higher, terrifying power?

Horror novels proposed that evil sometimes lived in plain sight. It was an unstoppable force. It lived in the hearts of men and women. It was there in the abnormal way I felt about girls. Evil lived in my eyes as they slipped over those bodice ripper covers and lingered on the breasts. It was a terrifying thing. It was a demonic possession.

Much like the Bible verses we read every week, these books held patterns of repeated behavior. The killer always comes back. The monster is never really dead. The things that haunt you hang around, not truly vanquished. Just lying in wait.

Hey, that's why we have sequels. Even Jesus rose three days later.

ꕤ

So there we stood in the bathroom. In the dark. Chanting. It was fun to huddle like that, breathing in each other's air and wondering what might happen. There were infinite possibilities. I touched my friends' hands and our fingers laced together. I liked how smooth their skin felt. My heart fluttered; skipped a beat. I understood that the scariest parts of myself were the things I couldn't exorcise. We flipped on the lights and our hands flew apart. We screamed.

There was no Mary there. Just three girls, terrified.

We laughed, glad it was done and that it was still only us. Then we went back to the living room and to our books, ready to scare ourselves a little more. Happy to hold fear comfortably in our palms, if only for a short while.

GODDAMN WEREWOLVES

AARON WINSLOW

I'll admit it: the whole scenario seems unlikely. A year ago, nobody would have believed that the solution to global warming would also turn every person on Earth into a werewolf. But that's exactly what happened.

I'm not talking about sprouting a little extra hair and getting the urge to growl after a good meal. The transformation was more substantial than that. But we didn't turn into sexy fetish werewolves either. No, after the transformation was complete everyone looked like a campy, bargain-basement Halloween-costume, Lon-Chaney-Jr.-in-*The-Wolfman*-style werewolf.

Maybe it was all worth it to solve global warming. This is actually a pretty healthy debate right now, and a lot of people a whole heck of a lot smarter than I am have weighed in on it, so I'm not even about to try. That's above my pay grade.

What exactly *is* my pay grade? And *why*, exactly, am I writing this? Doesn't everyone on Earth already know that they are a werewolf and thus have no need for narrative exposition? Well, yes and no, but that's beside the point. Let's just say this message is for the stars.

My name is Randy ~~Feldman~~ Wolfman and I'm currently barreling through the outer reaches of the solar system at 17 kilometers per second. You see, I'm an astronaut. Or, rather, an astro-wolf, as we now call them. I'm part of Elon Were-Musk's first were-manned mission into the void of space. It's a one-way ticket, as far as I can tell. There's no plan to colonize another planet or establish a permanent space station. Nope, I just shoved my were-ass into a spaceship designed and built by some shitty rich were-dude with no were-public oversight or responsibility and let 'er rip.

Normally, nobody would go along with something like this. Or, at least, the only people who would've volunteered would be real losers. But now, everyone's like, "Fuck it, I'm a werewolf, nothing makes sense, so I guess I'll just shoot myself into space."

At least, that was my way of thinking. Sure, being a werewolf *sounds* cool. And for a little while, it was. Have you ever had werewolf sex? Or been to a werewolf party? Even an all-werewolf baseball game is pretty damn exciting, although it remains a thinking wolf's game of statistics.

But surrendering to your canine urges gets old after a while. And, unfortunately, turning into a werewolf didn't do much for my were-anxiety and were-depression. In fact, it only made things worse!

Picture this: there you are, walking down the street, a week away from the full moon so you say to yourself, "Today's the day I get some shit done. No crazy werewolf antics. No binge feasting. I'll see the pack tomorrow. Today, I'm finally gonna start that novel. The great American werewolf novel."

And then *boom*. From out of nowhere, 10 of your friends jump out of the bushes.

"Time to go crazy, motherwolfer," they shout at you. "We're all werewolves! Goddamn fucking werewolves!"

"Not today," you say, and try to slip around the pack. "I need some time to write and chill."

But they pull you right back in and shove you around in a jocular yet aggressive way.

"'Write and chill'? That's loser human talk. We're werewolves now! We don't know why, but we are. And that means that we never need to chill. We only need to go crazy and live forever!"

Then they crack a cold one and hand it to you and your day's shot.

Fun? You bet. How could it not be, especially when you're a werewolf, which I most certainly am. But meaningful? Not exactly.

I think that gives you a pretty good idea of the day-to-day here on Were-Earth. So maybe that explains why, when I saw a flyer on the bulletin board of my favorite coffee shop, Howlin' Beans, asking for volunteers for a "Cool Space Mission." I tore the ticket off and used the free wi-fi to send an email straight to Elon Were-Musk.

And the rest, as they say, is were-history. All my were-buddies were supportive. At first, when I told them I was taking off, they were like, "What? Everything is so cool here, why would you leave? Where are you gonna go?"

"I'm gonna shoot myself into space and never come back."

They broke out classic were-smiles: "Hell yeah, motherwolfer. Fuck space. Why does it get to be all big and empty? Go out there and tear it up."

I think about that moment all the time out here as I careen into the void of the universe. Am I, at long last, getting some peace and quiet? Or am I just inadvertently spreading this basic-ass werewolf shit across the galaxy? I don't know the answer to that question.

You probably have some other questions, too. Like: How, and for how long, will I survive? What do I do to stay sane? If werewolf transformation is tied to the lunar cycle, why am I still a werewolf now that I'm well past the influence of Were-Earth's moon?

And, really, those questions are just the tip of the iceberg. But I'll level with you: I don't have a clue about any of this. Because I'm just a werewolf. A goddamn fucking werewolf.

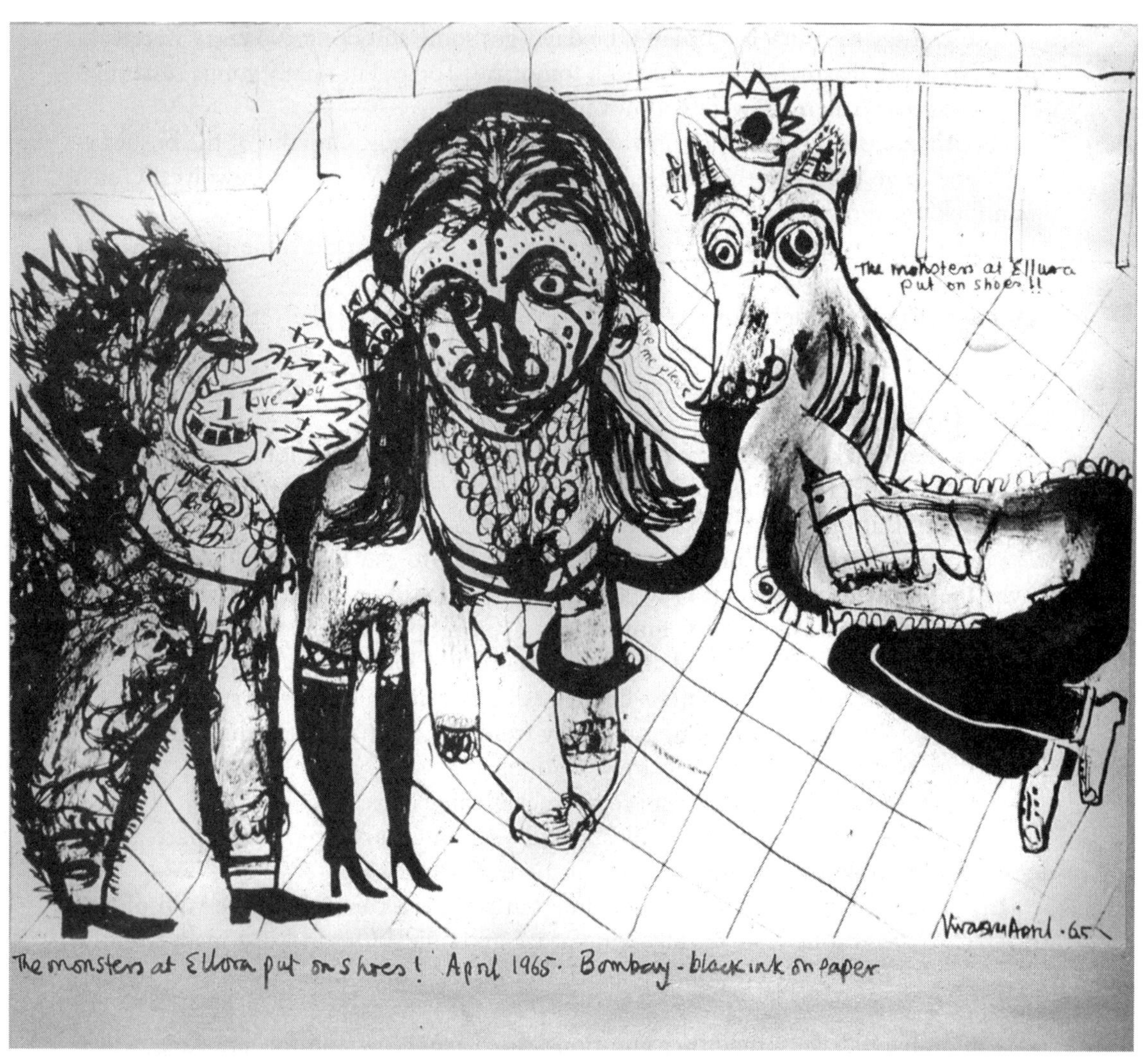

Vivan Sundaram, *The Monsters at Ellora Put on Shoes!*, 1965. Black ink on paper. Image courtesy of the artist

A PALACE OF WAITING ROOMS: LEGEND

VANESSA ANGÉLICA VILLARREAL

Anomaly
n. 1. a rupture; 2. a wailing sound that streaks the sky.

An Emily
n. 1. future daughter; 2. an aberration; 3. a collection of moving parts fluent in expectation

Aurora
n. 1. an electrical phenomenon characterized by the appearance of streamers of light in the womb; 2. literary goddess of the dawn; 3. fairy story Talia, mother of the twins Sun & Moon, originator of binaries

Barrenness/Baroness
n. 1. the state of being barren; 2. female subjects who habitually fail to fruit; 3. devoid or lacking interest or charm; 4. a woman of high social stature who owns land, property; 5. a woman flaking into dust

Blastocyst
n. 1. rain floods a moat in the perimeter; 2. white roots wind into black soil

Beauty/Belle
adj cum n. a woman trapped in paper

Cinderella
n. scrubbing & scrubbing & scrubbing all day

Colostrum
n. 1. a handful of seeds tossed into the spring night sky

Dystocia
n. too small hips, too short mother, too long labor, too high a weight, too high blood sugar, too painful the break, too large the child, too cursed the bloodline

Embryo
n. 1. young animal; 2. to leap

Fetal Distress
n. It would have been an easy labor had the Patient developed contractions. Patient was unresponsive to Pitocin during labor. Caesarean became only.

Fairy Godmother
n. The ceremony will go like this: place your tooth in the bowl and hold the lump of granite in your left hand. Unravel the rope and begin to eat the strands. With each strand you swallow, imagine your belly swelling, a thunderstorm igniting the walls of your sex.

Guinevere
n. 1. Welsh White Enchantress, White Fay; 2. a woman crowned with light at the foot of the altar, her back a knot of braids, her sex a knot of braids. 3. a woman abducted on horseback, limbs tied with rope to the hindquarters of a horse, ropes criss-crossed on her wrists for her infidelity to the king

Gestation
n. 1. a planet of belief emerging from the black; 2. SEE ONCE THE PATIENT, pg. 1

Hindmilk
n. nonexistent

Hyperemesis Gravidarum
n. The patient has continued to experience nausea & vomiting post-partum. Tests show that post-partum hormonal levels are normal & that nausea is highly irregular. Patient refuses meals.

In Vitro Fertilization
n. 1. Latin in glass; 2. The girl's hair spins crystal in the glass jar she is kept in, her dress drenched in descent into milksea. The girl is a stain in the panties of her mother. The girl is a voice in the glass, willing itself into existence.

Labyrinth
n. The prince fights against the infinite walls of the labyrinth to arrive at the entrance to the palace, & in the walls finds himself staring back at himself staring back at himself staring back at himselfselfhim at back staring himself at back staring himself at back & all the princes grow tails or wings or fins & rush.

(Mis)carriage
n. The princess arrives in a (mis)carriage pulled by four white horses, yanking their heads back as they exit the dense fog. The (mis)carriage is adorned in sound & song, swallowed up by the sand beneath.

Ogre
n. In the kingdom, all the wars rage on in the realms of the ogre and the violence echoes off the stones.

Ovarian Hyperstimulation Syndrome
n. A condition caused by speaking prayers inside of dolls. Often seen in women aged three to 45. Behaviors may cause spontaneous generation of fluid, but salt may be swallowed to forestall the effects of loneliness.

Placenta
n. There are telephones crowding every inch of the walls of the palace, each directly connected to the palace's servant staff. Some servants press their bodies up against the walls attempting to divine which of the phones will connect to the outside.

Rapunzel
n. 1. Fairy story. the fruit that brings wishes to life; 2. the condition that fertility be surrendered at birth

Trial of Labor
v. Some girls are born princesses and some girls are born servants; some mothers are queens and some mothers are cattle; 2. SEE *Madrigal v. Quilligan*

Zygote
n. a question in the water; 2. a balance.

Raha Raissnia, *Shade*, 2018. Oil, pigment, gel medium on canvas. 39 x 67 1/2 inches
Courtesy of the artist and Miguel Abreu Gallery, New York. Photo: Stephen Faught

ALL INCLUDED

PAUL LA FARGE

— Ghosts? Alida said. In an old house like this, probably.

Robert was only joking, but he had expected a less equivocal answer. — I see. Is that why…?

— The price? Alida laughed. — Oh, honey, no. That's called divorce. And it's winter, you're smart to be buying in the winter.

— I see, Robert said again. And the furniture?

— Not included! But if you want it, I can ask the seller. I don't know where she thinks it will all go.

— Thanks, but no.

— New broom, Alida said. Just what an old house needs. Look, here's a cedar closet for your coats and sweaters and things.

Half an hour later, Robert shook Alida's oddly warm hand, got into his car, and found his way to the Taconic. He wanted the house. Who wouldn't want it? A historic three-bedroom farmhouse on five acres of land, hundreds of feet above sea level, and relatively close to the city! By the time he reached Westchester, Robert was daydreaming, masochistically, about being outbid by vile hedgies who would lay glass tile in the shower, or crypto-bros who'd hold shamanic rituals in the woods. He called Alida from the Bronx and said he was ready to make an offer.

— Wow, okay, love at first sight?

— It's a good place, Robert said stiffly.

Four busy weeks later, the house belonged to Robert. He drove up to take possession on a Friday afternoon, bringing with him a few things that would come in handy. But his first emotion, on opening what was now his side door, and stepping into his mud room, was disappointment. Now that the furniture was gone, the rooms looked smaller than he remembered, and less bright. The floor bulged, as though trying to contain something that was trying to come up from below. The charming Revolutionary stairs were crooked, the paint on their treads badly scratched. Robert touched the ovoid complexities that ran along the underside of the dining-room mantel: original woodwork, Alida had affirmed. Carved in the days when the ink wasn't dry on the Constitution. He tried to project his mind back into that time, to feel the thrill of the American experiment as the people who lived here then might have felt it, but what he actually felt was that the previous owners' furniture might be gone, but its smell remained: cat pee and Febreze. He opened one of the beautiful twelve-paned windows and let in a slab of frigid air.

When he looked in the living room, he saw that the previous owners' furniture was not, in fact, entirely gone. A loveseat and a rocking chair remained: the chair by the front windows, the loveseat at an angle to the fireplace. Robert wondered if the seller had left them behind for *him*. More likely she'd run out of room in the moving truck, and guessed it wouldn't be worth his while to complain. And she was right, he thought, but still. Away with you! He lifted the rocking chair, with the idea that he'd stick it in the basement, but it was strangely heavy, as if its frame were reinforced with lead. It didn't matter. Robert would come back with guys — guys would remove it. On his way out of the room he noticed a third item that had been left behind: an iron lawn jockey which functioned as a doorstop, keeping the living-room door open. He scowled at it. It grinned indifferently.

— You're going, too, he said.

He went out to the car and brought in his supplies. The easel, the precious Audubon, the tackle box with his watercolors and inks. A box of kitchen things and some meager groceries from the gas-station deli on Route 9. A beat-up but still warm ski jacket, which he hung in the cedar closet. A pair of binoculars. On his last trip in, he saw that it had begun to snow. He set up the easel in the little south-facing room he'd marked out as his studio, and spent a while turning it one way and another. When it got dark he went downstairs. The snow fell heavily now: he could see it swirling outside the kitchen windows. Robert had planned to drive on to the house of some old friends who lived in the Catskills, but the thought of attempting their mountain road at night, in a snowstorm, discouraged him. Why chance it? He called his friends to say he wasn't coming; they did not sound disappointed, or even, he thought, particularly surprised.

Robert heated a can of minestrone in the pot he'd brought from the city, buttered two slices of un-toasted bread, and took the meal into the living room. He sat in the rocking chair and watched snowflakes halo a white-blue streetlamp up the road. What did people do here in the winter, he wondered. He pictured a fire in the fireplace, a frocky Revolutionary family singing along with an odd tortoiseshell piano, only he didn't know any songs from the period, so their music was a jumble of Christmas carols and "The Star-Spangled Banner." He washed his dishes with fragrant gas-station-deli dish soap, brushed his teeth, and lay down on the loveseat to check his phone. It, the loveseat, was too short, but if he drew his knees up it became tolerable. The problem was the cushion, which stank of farts and dust. If only he had something to spray it with, he thought, and chuckled at his own foolishness and snobbery. That was when the ghost came in. She was black, which was almost as surprising to Robert as her being a ghost at all.

She was much younger than Robert, was his next thought. Thirty at most. She wore a long brown dress and a blue apron. Her hair was tied back under a neat yellow kerchief.

— You shouldn't have let the fire go out, she said.

— Sorry, Robert said.

— Never mind, the ghost said. Only my knees hurt when it's cold like this. Looks like it's going to snow all night.

— How can you tell?

— No wind, and there's a smell in the air, can't you smell it? A heavy smell.

— Maybe. Robert smelled only sofa cushion.

— There, the ghost said, without having done anything visible. She rose to her feet.

— Will you need anything else?

— Have you got a bed? Robert was delighted by his failure to be shocked, unless this *was* shock.

— You want a bed down here?

— No, never mind. What's your name?

— Anna.

— Have you been here long, Anna?

— Yes, a while.

— I just moved in, Robert said. I'm Robert.

Anna curtsied. Before he could say anything else, she was gone: carried out of the room on quiet ghostly feet. Robert lay still, almost not breathing, not because he was afraid of the ghost — he still wasn't — but because he was afraid of inconveniencing her by making her come back in. This is extremely strange, he thought, but he was the one who had brought up ghosts in the first place, so he couldn't claim to be entirely surprised. And it was nice, in a way, to imagine that he wasn't alone.

༄

The snow was impassable the next morning. Robert's car, seen from the house, was a white lump. He boiled water, made a mug of fancy Ethiopian coffee and wondered what to do. He remembered seeing a shovel on the porch, but if it had been there once, it was gone now. The storm had left bitter cold air behind, and gusts of wind that kicked up the stinging dry snow. Robert hurried back in and stood in the mud room, rubbing his frozen hands. He'd have to call for help. Fortunately, there was a phone book in the coat closet, a fat yellow phone book, practically a historic artifact. Robert looked up "Snow Removal" and made a round of calls, but no one answered. He left his number, trying not to sound too desperate, or too out-of-town. He went down to the basement to look for that shovel, and was surprised to find, in the jumble of paint cans and nail-bearing boards which the previous owner had left behind, a low red bookcase full of paperbacks. They were all mysteries, Robert saw, and practically all by the same person, a writer he'd never heard of named Towers Wick. Their titles all had *Death* in them: *Death of an Average Joe*, *Death Takes Ten*, *Death Doubles Down*. Robert was not a mystery reader; he liked the classics, Balzac, Dickens, Conrad, Henry James. Still, beggars, et cetera. He took a much-used copy of *Death, All Included* up to the living room, and, with an easy feeling that the house was looking out for him, settled in the rocking chair and waited for the snow-removal people to call.

Death, All Included was set in one of those hermetic Caribbean resorts that Robert had instinctually avoided all his life: a compound of tawny cement bungalows against a background of mangrove swamps, a white beach and sparkling blue water all the way to the horizon. The main characters were Rex, a portly old detective, and his young assistant, Archie; they were on vacation. They did what vacationing people do: sat on the veranda and watched the ocean, hunted for seashells, fussed over the food. Inevitably, a dead body was going to show up, and their holiday would become an investigation, but meanwhile, for pages and pages, nothing much happened. Rex argued with the chef about the béarnaise sauce. Archie took a snorkeling lesson. They both smoked and drank as if no one would ever get cancer. Ah, the '50s, Robert thought. He wondered if *Death, All Included* was a late volume in the Towers Wick *corpus*, and he, Wick, was toying deliberately with the reader's expectations.

Anna was wiping a ghostly rag along the windowsills.

— Oh! Robert said. I didn't see you come in.

— Just tidying up. Will you be wanting dinner?

Robert thought it was early to be asking about dinner, then remembered that in Anna's era it had been the midday meal. — No, thanks, he said. I'm hoping to be on my way before then.

— So soon?

— Actually, I was supposed to leave last night, my friends are expecting me. Anna …

— Yes?

— Why are *you* here? The question had occurred to him the night before.

— Why do you think? Anna said.

Robert felt suddenly that he had entered uncertain territory. — I suppose there's something you have to do, he said. Some task you left unfinished when you were … Could he say *alive*? Call a ghost a ghost? — Earlier, he concluded.

Anna laughed sharply. — There's always something to do in an old house like this.

When she had left, silently, insubstantially, Robert got his phone and verified what he had suspected to be the case, that New York State had permitted slavery until 1827, decades after this house was built. If Anna had been here since the beginning — if she had died, as was probable, in her '20s or '30s — then she might have died a slave, and, by some ghastly metaphysics, she might be one still. The question was, what to do about it?

Free ghost slave, Robert typed into his phone, but the internet was useless for this. Probably you had to call a priest, to arrange an exorcism. Robert scowled. He had known some priests as a child and his memories of them were not good. Anyway, he thought, these people would have been Protestants. Wouldn't they? Soon he was daydreaming about having people to dinner. *Yes, she's a real ghost. Of an enslaved person. Did you know, slavery was legal in New York until 1827? Just about every household up here had a slave or two. A reminder that you Northerners are hardly guiltless.*

Robert was hungry. He heated a can of black bean soup and ate it standing up, in the kitchen, then he pulled on his coat and city shoes and went outside. The snow, it turned out, was deep but light. He could wade through it, kicking up sprays of glittering crystals as he went, leaving a clear track behind. His car was good and buried, but he brushed snow from the windshield with his sleeve, and determined that it would take only a few minutes to clear the rest of it. He went back into the house, took off his shoes, and was suddenly overcome by the desire to lie down. He hadn't slept well the night before, and he hadn't eaten well, either. He sank onto the loveseat, picked up *Death, All Included*. Apparently Towers Wick had known something about tropical fish, and he wanted you to know it, too: there were pages and pages of Archie snorkeling, in the company of amberjacks and African pompanos, French angelfish and cocoa damselfish. When he came out of the water, Rex was nowhere to be seen. A crime! Robert thought, but no. Rex had thrown out his back carrying a beach umbrella. He was getting a massage from Clarence, the physical therapist. His large buttocks trembled under a threadbare white towel. Ah, realism, Robert thought. The triumph of the superfluous detail. Only what did it triumph over? Lightning, pirate ships, tombs with bloody hands rising out of them, a terrible pair of eyes — before Robert knew it, he was asleep.

☙❧

When he woke up, it was nearly dark, and icy rain thwapped the windows. Robert felt suddenly desperate to be gone from this place. Why was he still here, what had happened to his real life? He stuffed a few things irritably into a gym bag, turned down the heat, switched off the lights. But his shoes had been ruined: drenched in melted snow and left beside the baseboard heater, they had curled up like clown shoes. He couldn't even put them on — something was wrong with the width. Ridiculous, he thought. Shoes in hand, he opened the front door, and stepped, in his socks, into the slush, but at this point it occurred to him that he was about to do something stupid. Even if he could stand outside long enough to free the car, was he going to drive back to the city in wet socks? He went back in. He'd packed his kitchen things in newspaper but he now stuffed it into his shoes, and used his fork and knife as straighteners. He changed his socks: already his toes were red with cold. If he'd stayed out any longer, he'd probably have got frostbite. He turned the heat back up.

— Well, Anna, I guess it's you and me, he said.

Anna came around a corner, on the far side of which, so far as Robert knew, there was only a wall. — Did you want something?

— Roast chicken for dinner tonight.

— You mean, for supper? I'll see what we have in the cold room.

Anna vanished again. Cold room? Did the house have a cold room? Maybe in the days when all the rooms had been cold.

— Come back, Robert said. I was just kidding.

But Anna could not be kidded like that. Robert heated a can of chili vegetable soup and ate it with his sole remaining utensil, the spoon. He washed up. His shoes were still not dry and by the sound of it the icy rain was still going strong, so he withdrew to the living room, to the rocking chair, which was beginning to feel like *his* chair, the way a restaurant you visit twice on a vacation starts to feel like *your* restaurant. He opened *Death, All Included* to where he'd left off. Archie and Rex sat in the hotel's dining room, watching the waiters nail sheets of plywood over the French windows. A hurricane was coming, but Clarence, who doubled as the headwaiter, had told them not to worry. The island got hurricanes all the time. Tomorrow, he said, you're going to see some big waves! Tonight, enjoy your dinner. It was some sort of flat fish, haphazardly sautéed, with cherry tomatoes, iceberg lettuce, and a basket of chewy dinner rolls. Served with an inferior Chablis, Rex noted, disapprovingly.

— Give them a break, Archie said. They're all on hurricane duty.

— What? I can't hear you over this infernal hammering.

— Give them a break, Archie said.

— Absolutely not, Rex said. This is *my* break. They may take theirs at another time.

— You're a curmudgeon, Archie said.

— What?

— Never mind. I'm going out for a smoke.

— I'll join you.

They went out. The sky was black, over a black ocean. The wind had not yet picked up. A couple of young boys were carrying the umbrellas in.

— Looks like the end of the world out there, Archie said.

— Not likely, Rex said. Although I'd rather perish than eat whatever they're serving for dessert.

— I'll bet you would, Archie said. How long are we going to stay here, anyway? I've chatted up all the eligible women, and nothing doing. The fish, likewise.

— Perhaps you should focus on the pleasures of the mind.

— In a place like this?

— Certainly, Rex said. For instance, have you noticed that the ashtrays in our room are emptied four times a day? At ten, noon, four, and six.

— Great. If any of our ashes go missing, I'll know where to look.

— Will you? Do you know who empties them? That boy there. He also puts fresh flowers in that ugly blue vase on the dresser.

Archie sighed. — From which you conclude…?

— Nothing, except that this hotel is understaffed. But I *notice*, Archie. There can be no rest from noticing.

Their conversation continued, but Robert didn't follow it. He was thinking about what made a world — the same question he'd asked in his prize-winning book, thirty years ago. How did a story become a world? Did it have to contain pointless conversa-

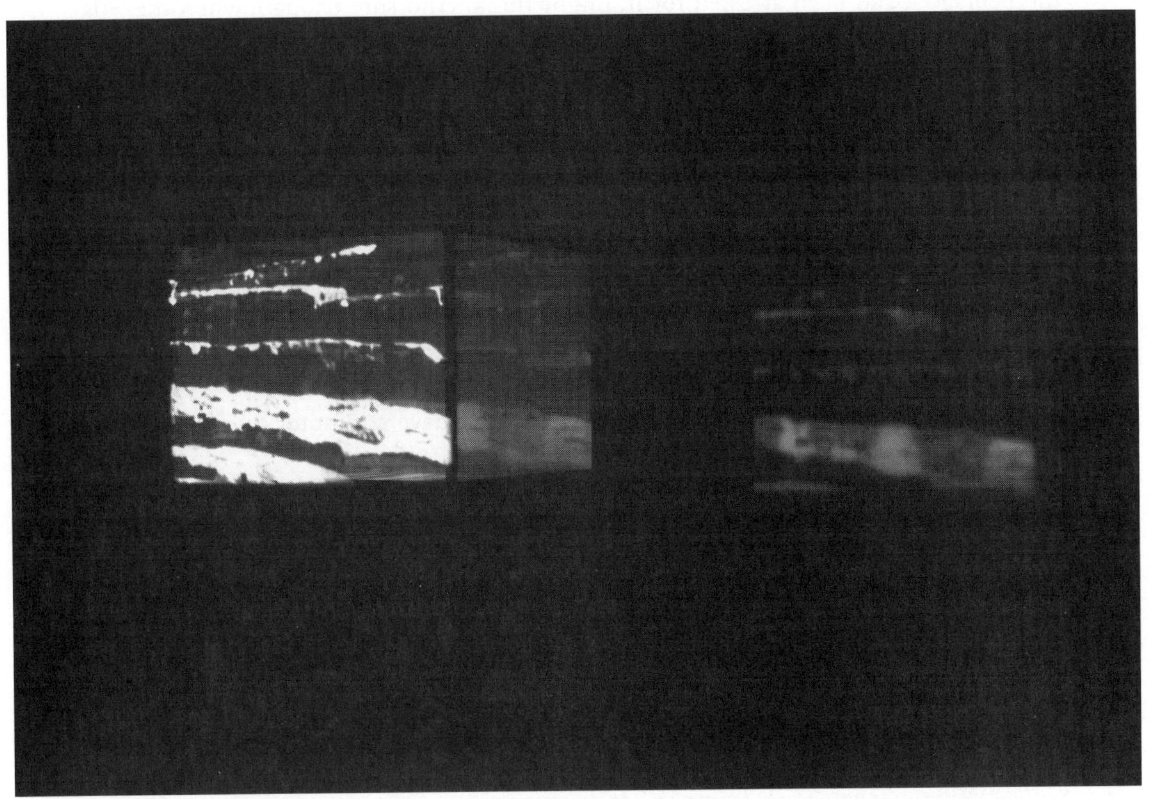

Raha Raissnia, *Galvanoscope 1*, 2018. Projector, 16mm film, wood, scrim. 3 min. loop. Sculpture dimensions: 23 x 31 x 31 inches. Overall installation dimensions variable. Edition of 2 + 1 AP. Courtesy the artist and Miguel Abreu Gallery, New York. Photo: Stephen Faught

tions, superfluous details? Did you have to be able to draw a map of it, like Yoknapatawpha County? In his book, Robert had argued that a story became a world when it contained the possibility of meaningful action, with the emphasis on *possibility*: no one had to do anything, but you had to believe that they could. Having a world, he'd argued, was the opposite of being helpless. Looking back, there was something very Vietnam War-y about his thesis: it was what a young man who'd once climbed the fence outside the Pentagon, and been arrested for it, might think. And sure enough, when the '90s rolled around and the grounds of the conversation shifted to that other question, *who* acts, Robert's book had not become objectionable so much as it became irrelevant. Robert still taught from it; the angry young man he had been died hard. But he was already shifting his grounds, too, becoming involved in the university's administration. It had been years since it occurred to him to ask, seriously, what makes a world? Now he wondered if a world was something that shut something else out. But what? Another world?

— Anna! he called.

— Yes?

— Do you have a minute?

— Just.

Robert wondered at that. How could a ghost not have a minute? She'd been here for centuries.

— I want to help you, he said. Is there something I can do?

— Can you cook?

— Yes, Robert said, as a matter of fact. But that's not what I mean. I want to release you from this work you're doing.

— You want to let me go?

— I want to free you, Anna. You should have a life of your own. Or an afterlife, I don't know how these things work.

— Who are you? Anna said.

— I don't know what you mean.

— Where do you come from? What do you do?

— I'm from Charlotte, North Carolina, originally. I live in New York. I am about to retire from a very well-respected university.

Robert wondered if she could hear the irony in that last phrase. Probably it was hard to respect any place when you knew how people ran it.

— Why are you here?

— To enjoy some peace in my old age, Robert said, and meant it.

Anna looked at him squarely. — Tomorrow is my day off, she said. Do you need anything before I go?

— No, Robert said. He felt strangely flattened by their conversation. Thank you, Anna.

— All right, Anna said. Be careful if you go outside, the steps are icy.

ᘓᘐ

Robert slept well that night, and woke up with a hard-on. The rain had stopped; the sky was a deep clear blue, an almost contrite blue, hiding nothing. Branches sparkled in the low yellow sunlight. Robert peed, and his erection went away, but that was all right. He was alive, life was everywhere, he was full of life! He was, however, running low on food. Fortunately, his shoes were once again shoe-shaped. He put them on, went out, slipped on the porch steps, which were sheeted in transparent ice, fell, and landed painfully on his coccyx and the middle of his back. He lay there for a bit, the breath knocked out of him, then clutched the railing and tried to stand. The sun had melted the skin of the ice, and his leather-soled city shoes got no traction. His back twinged ominously. In the end he crawled back into the house, and sat, aching and humbled, on the mud-room floor. He would have to call someone, but who? For some reason he thought of Bernard, all cozy in Narragansett, but Bernard despised him now. Anyway, what could Bernard do? Better to call an ambulance, although he doubted they could get up the steps. Call the police, the fire department? They would laugh at him for years.

— Anna! he shouted.

The ghost did not appear. Of course not: it was Sunday, her day off.

With his hand on the small of his back, Robert lurched into the living room and lowered himself into the rocking chair. Ravens hopped on the icy lawn, calling hoarsely to one another. Robert had no desire to sketch them, although he'd heard ravens were very intelligent, and remembered the wrongs that had been done to them from one generation to the next. Unless these were crows? His ankle throbbed; pulling up his pants leg, he saw that it was swelling. What a mess.

Worse, he'd forgotten to charge his phone; now the battery was nearly dead. This was, he thought, a very old situation. Survival. Not that *his* survival was in doubt: he'd call the police the moment there was any real danger. In the meantime he could play at feeling what previous occupants of the house had surely felt, the tightening of necessity, the need to plan, and to act. He took off his sock and wrapped it around his ankle, as a bandage. As soon as he could walk, he'd look in the freezer: surely there was ice. He'd ice his back. He'd make it to the gas-station deli, and someone there would help him. Groaning, he shifted from the chair to the loveseat, and elevated his bandaged foot. He was a pioneer, he was a frontiersman…For lack of anything better to do while his body repaired itself, he picked up *Death, All Included.*

He must have read several pages without paying attention the night before, or else Towers Wick was skipping ahead. The hurricane had blown over. The kids were prying the boards off the dining-room windows, while Archie and Rex watched from the veranda. It was windy outside but not unpleasant: almost like autumn. The beach was strewn with shards of dense white foam. Suddenly Archie put his Bloody Mary down on the white iron table.

— Look!

He pointed at the surf. Something black lay in it: a log, or maybe a porpoise.

— Someone's drowned, Archie said. Care to investigate?

— I'm eating, Rex said. You go in and find a doctor.

The staff were busy polishing furniture and mopping the marble floors. No one stood at the concierge's desk. Finally, Archie found Clarence in a service corridor, pushing a dolly stacked with crates of still-clicking lobsters.

— Clarence, is there a doctor handy? I think somebody's drowned.

— No, Clarence said, ours is helping at the clinic.

— Dammit. Come on, let's see if there's anything you and I can do.

Rex had already gone down to the water to investigate. They followed: sure enough, it was a body, a human body. A black man in tan pants, no shirt, one brown shoe. How he had drowned was a mystery, but it looked as if he had been in the water for some time. Now the surf rolled him from side to side, like a restless sleeper.

— He's dead, Clarence said.

— Clearly, Rex said. You'd better call the police.

— Yes, sir.

Archie poked at the body with his foot. Horrible to imagine fish eating a body. And then you ate the fish. And then…He helped the body to flop over, and studied its face. No particular expression, no sign of foul play. He was, had been, younger than he looked at first.

— Maybe he fell out of a boat, Clarence said.

— Could be. Come on, Archie.

— Hold on. You're leaving the scene of a crime?

— Do you see anyone around here who's going to write me a check?

— No.

— Then come on. My eggs have surely become inedible.

❧

Blue evening, and Robert couldn't stand up. Something was wrong with his middle back: the injured muscles had frozen and set. Or had he fractured a vertebra? Even lifting his head caused him to grimace with pain. Survival, he thought, survival! But his phone didn't work at all.

— Anna! he shouted.

This time, thank god, she came in.

— Yes?

— I need your help. I've hurt my back, and I can't move.

— Slipped on the steps?

— Yes.

— All right, let me fix you up a liniment.

When Anna came back holding a tin bowl, he felt improbably relieved.

— Can you turn over? she asked.

Painfully, with great effort, he could. Anna sat beside him on the edge of the love-seat.

— I was thinking, she said. Do you really want to do something for me?

— Of course I do.

— Then burn this house down.

— What?

— Burn it down.

Without thinking, Robert said, — But I just moved in!

— No, you didn't, Anna said. All there is, is this stinky loveseat and a chair, and *him*. She pointed at the lawn jockey. — And they're not even yours. You have insurance, right?

— Sure, but … Robert was at a loss. Finally he arrived at: — Where would I go?

— You can go back to New York. Or Charlotte. Wherever you like.

— But I don't want to, Robert said, peevishly.

— Well then, Anna said. She floated to her feet.

So this was a negotiation. — What if I write you a certificate, Robert said.

— Who would read it?

— I don't know, Anna. I told you, I don't understand how these things work. What if I bring a lawyer over, or a minister?

— Ha, Anna said.

— At least let me look into it. Maybe there's something we're missing, here. Another way out.

— You can look, Anna said. She drifted toward the door.

Christ almighty, Robert thought, I'm being blackmailed by a ghost. But he really didn't want her to leave, not while he needed her help.

— Fine, he said, I'll do it.

— Do you promise?

— I promise.

A hand, a ghostly hand, lifted the back of Robert's shirt. His back was salved with a greasy lotion that smelled of rosemary and burnt hair.

— Better?

Robert wriggled. The pain in his back was less. He rolled over, sat up. Anna was already at the door.

— Remember, she said, and went out.

Robert hopped to the kitchen and plugged in his phone. It was inexplicable, he thought. Could Anna really have helped him? More likely he'd dreamed her and her weird salve. The body was capable of remarkable changes while asleep. People woke up, their hair all suddenly white…He did remember what he had promised Anna, but he had no serious thought of carrying it out. Why would he burn down a perfectly good house? He'd free her by other means, if she was real, and could be freed. A certificate. A priest, holy water, that mumbo-jumbo.

For some reason he thought of Mara Owen-Jones, who had been a junior professor in his department, some years back. She had come up for tenure, and Robert had fought for her, even though her book — on Dumas *père*, had it been? — was a turgid mess of critical jargon. We need her perspective, he'd told the dean — this was before Robert *was* the dean. The students want it. And *we* need it, too, even if we don't all admit that we do. — And what is her perspective? the dean asked him. Robert wondered if the dean was putting him on. Unforgivably, he had blushed. — The African-American perspective, he'd said. The perspective of a descendant of slaves, of oppressed people. — Is she? the dean had asked, and, truly, Robert had had no idea. — But come on, Robert said, you aren't going to suggest that there's no such thing as the African-American perspective? — I didn't say that, the dean said, smiling faintly, maliciously. — I just want you to tell me what it is.

Robert had botched it. Ask Mara, he ought to have said. Or just read *Invisible Man*. Instead he'd tried to answer the question. In the end, it hadn't mattered much: while the dean dragged his feet, Mara had taken a job in, Robert thought, Minnesota. To this day, her books continued to appear. I tried, though, he thought. You can't say I didn't try. His foot was too swollen to fit into his shoe, but it didn't matter. He called his friends in the Catskills, and explained, in the least alarming way possible, his situation. They promised to jump in the car momentarily. And that's that, Robert thought. I survive. He sat in the rocking chair to wait. Because it was still there, he picked up *Death, All Included* — and it welcomed him in.

The police had come and gone. The body was at the morgue, waiting for somebody to claim it. In short, everything was back in order, except Archie, who moped on the veranda, smoking a cigarette and staring at the ocean as if it were a suspect.

— Come in, Rex said, we don't want to hold up the kitchen.

— In a minute, Archie said.

— You can't punish me like this, Rex said. It's not my fault that young man died. Nor is it my job to figure out who killed him, if anyone did.

— I know all that.

— Then why are you being so awful?

— Forget it, Archie said, throwing his cigarette into the sand. It'll pass.

— It had better, Rex said. Come on. I suggested some adjustments to the béarnaise, and you have to tell me if it's palatable.

They went in. Robert watched them from the veranda: a strange couple, he thought, but who was he to judge? Most people were strange. He rattled the ice in his glass and wondered what he would do that evening, then his attention was caught by a figure walking on the beach, at the edge of the tide. She wore a dark blue dress, but otherwise she looked exactly like Anna.

— Anna! he shouted.

How strange that she had turned up here, he thought, with a surge of real pleasure: just when he'd thought there would be no one to talk to!

— Anna!

He stood at the railing of the veranda and waved. But, strangely, Anna, if it was Anna, paid him no attention. She walked slowly along the wet white sand, her head down, as though she were looking for something. Once, she knelt to inspect a patch of sand more closely, but so far as Robert could see, there was nothing there. Then she rose to her feet and kept walking.

Robert wondered if he should go down to her. But she must have heard him, must have seen him waving and practically making a fool of himself. It was a case of mistaken identity, he thought. He set his drink on the railing and went in. The dining room was full; Clarence, in his role as headwaiter, was chaperoning a stooped couple to a table by the French windows. Robert waved at him, but Clarence ignored him, too. For a moment Robert was certain that he had spoiled everything somehow: now no one would see him, now he would wait, and wait... The feeling quickly passed, though, and here came Clarence, beaming. He led Robert to a table at the far end of the room, next to a solitary man, a Cuban, maybe, or a Brazilian, who was reading a book. Robert felt a thrill of possibility. He was in a foreign country, and anything could happen, even if, in his experience, nothing ever did.

FICTIVE MATRIARCHIES

MAYA GURANTZ

A few years ago I inherited a library of feminist spiritualist literature from a dying woman, who had long been a follower of Dianic Wicca, a woman's-only offshoot of the neo-pagan movement. I'm afraid I didn't expect much from these stacks. I had never been interested in the sisterhood of new age witchcraft. I was embarrassed by the sincerity, the long jangly necklaces and beads and scarves and Stevie Nicks skirts. The aesthetic seemed frozen in time and place, specifically 1971 Los Angeles, where first Dianic Wiccan group (Susan B. Anthony Coven #1) was founded. I cringed in the shops that sold the accoutrement — as if Tarot Packs and crystals could blow open a door to the divine. I was suspicious of white women creating pagan lineages based in ethnic histories so often not their own.

When I received the books, I was already in the middle of reading *Les Évangiles des Quenouilles* (*The Distaff Gospels*), a popular 15th-century collection of "women's wisdom." This book resembles a shorter *Decameron*; it isn't set during the Italian plague but during the dead of winter when women would sit together over long, dark evenings spinning wool and exchanging advice, dirty jokes, and folk cures. The text is by turns delightful and painful: it exposes how "witchcraft," or what we call "witchcraft," often arose from womens' total political powerlessness. For women, control had to remain anchored in the realm of the symbolic, communicated through the use of stories, spells, and rituals fashioned with the items at hand (this is why witches are associated with broomsticks, cauldrons, and other kitchen objects). In *Les Évangiles des Quenouilles*, if you want your husband to love his children beyond all measure, trick him into washing his face with the baby's urine. Warn him that if a pregnant woman's food cravings are not satisfied, the baby might be born without a vital organ. If he kicks you while you're pregnant, find his shoe and drink from it to avoid a damaging birth. Magic reveals itself to be a tool for the basic survival and human dignity of women and children — defiant, creative, desperate. In my new books, I encountered some of the most radical second-wave feminism I had ever seen outside the *SCUM Manifesto.* It seemed like the spiritual realm allowed what the political realm repeatedly denied: women were free to clearly articulate their hunger to shape an entirely new reality free from male dominance.

One passage that struck me particularly came from Margot Adler's classic *Drawing Down the Moon: Witches, Druids, Goddess-Worshippers, and Other Pagans in America.* About ritual, Adler writes: "If dreams are how are unconscious mind speaks to our conscious mind, ritual is how our conscious mind can speak to our unconscious mind." Ritual establishes, asserts, inculcates values and beliefs, seeds them deeply within us. It may be the only we way we can alchemize our instincts and reframe deeply damaging social training. Mid-20th-century female occultist Dion Fortune described magic as the art of changing consciousness at will. In allowing us to transform our most inner selves and believe in new futures, ritual can be magic.

The following pieces are performance scores which represent the imagined rituals of a fictive matriarchy. They were developed with dancers over multiple residencies. In making them, I asked myself: What would the fictive matriarchy choose to commemorate? What values would we enact, as a group, through our bodies? I asked my performers — what did they wish to communicate consciously to their unconscious selves?

Feel free to learn and perform these scores. Use them to imagine creating your own. The project is ongoing.

This text is adapted from a chapbook released with the solo gallery show of the video documentation of these rituals at Greenleaf Gallery, Whittier, California, curated by Jenny Herrick. Special thanks to Hothouse Residency at UCLA World Arts and Culture Department, Lisa Channer and the students of the Theater/Dance Department at the University of Minnesota, the dancers of the University of Utah and MoCA Utah, and to Lise Patt and the Institute of Cultural Inquiry, where this project began.

Ritual for Accepting Death

Ritual by which, as a community, we learn not to fear death, but to accept it as a part of life.

1. Begins with Group in standing circle.

2. Group silently and collectively selects one member (❍) to encounter death — all but one walk behind her to signal her selection, except for the one facing her (✶), who remains.

3. ❍ and ✶ embrace, then step back while continuing to hold one another's hands or wrists.

4. ❍ falls back into the arms of the group.

5. Group lowers ❍ down to the ground and use the palms of their hands to brush her into the ground, until she relaxes entirely, signaled by a long exhale.

6. Once ❍ exhales, rest of group lies down around her in a tight cluster, all facing the same direction.

7. The group, remaining in a tight cluster, stands up and lies back down in a rippling wave that continues in a circular pattern, ending in the same initial cluster around ❍.

8. Pause.

9. Break.

2.

3.

5.

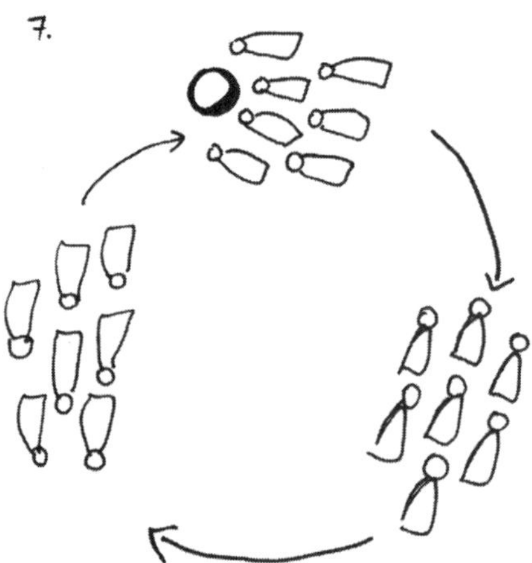

Ritual for Honoring the Difficulty of Goodbye

1. Start in group of 16 or eight. Everyone pairs up, embraces, and freezes in the embrace.

2. One member of each pair decides to be "A" and frees herself from the embrace in such a way that allows the other member, now "B," to remain in the frozen position.

3. From her frozen position, B melts into generating small movements based on whatever shape in which she has been left. This lasts until the end of the ritual.

3. All of the remaining "A" members, having freed themselves from their initial embrace, restart the process with one another.

4. They repeat this process of embracing and freeing until the final "freed" member remains.

5. Ritual breaks when final "freed" member walks away.

Ritual for Public Expression and Sharing of Rage

The community recognizes an individual member's rage, and shares it, to help her free it from her body and release it into the atmosphere.

1. Ritual initiated by one group member ♋.

2. ♋ runs to the center of the space, crouches, and begins tapping on a specific spot on the ground with her index finger as if to say, "Here, here, here, this is the problem, here, right here."

3. The rest of group runs in and joins her in a crouch, tapping at the same location, acknowledging the target of her anger.

4. Once everyone is tapping (as if to say, we are all witnessing together), ♋ begins to physically express her rage in a repeated gesture and sound that should not be premeditated.

5. The rest of the group imitates the gesture, repeating it with ♋. The group continues to perform this gesture, infusing it with more and more energy, until ♋ expresses that she's finished.

6. Break.

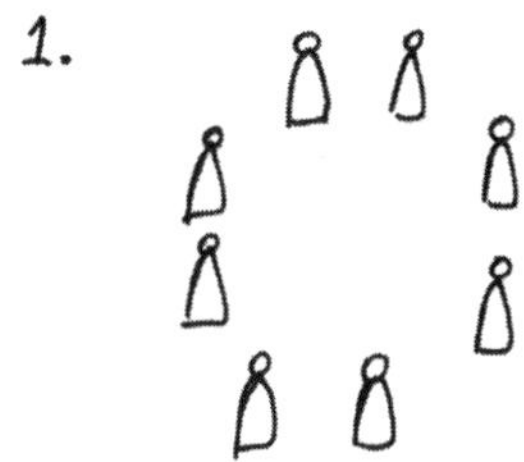

Ritual Reenacting Female Baby Joining Female Society

The word "gossip" originates from the term "god's sib," or "god's sibling" — essentially, a godparent — a close friend or family member upon whom one can depend for their child's care. The "gossiping" referred to a social event in which women would gather to attend the birth of a friend or relative, supporting the post-partum mother, sharing care of the new child, and telling stories. Negative connotations of "gossip" grew at times of heightened social misogyny, as a manner of undermining the value of women's speech and heightening the danger of women's speech in community.

In this ritual, we elevate the continuity of female community, as the female baby is born and comes into movement and communication with the female cluster.

1. Begins in standing circle.

2. One member (☽) silently decides to lead the ritual by stepping into the circle.

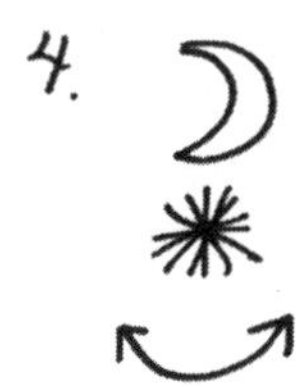

3. Person (✹) standing opposite from ☽ steps in, turns around and gets on her hands and knees, creating a "cradle" with her back.

4. ☽ curls up on ✹'s back, and is rocked back and forth three times.

5. ☽ rolls off of ✹'s back and comes to the ground.

6. The rest of the group (including ✹) immediately sits in a V-shape formation and, ignoring ☽ entirely, begins talking at the same time, loudly, enthusiastically: gossip, stories about their days.

7. While the group speaks, ☽ takes herself, slowly, through the stages of early physical development — stretching, curling into a ball, rolling over, pushing up on her hands, pushing up onto hands and knees, rocking back and forth.

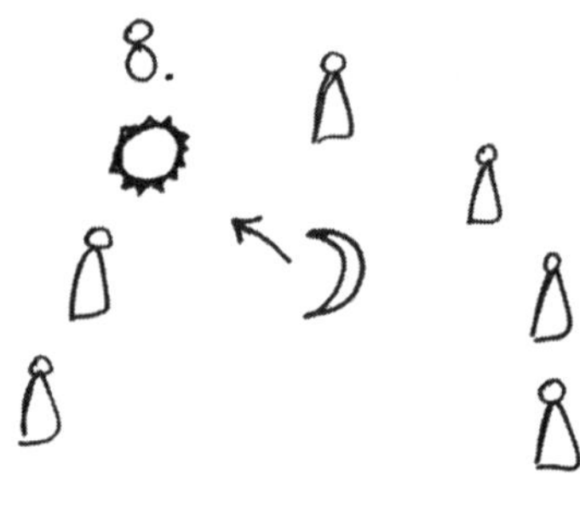

8. When ☽ manages to push herself into seated position, the Group falls silent. ☽ selects a member of the group (☼), reaching her arms out to her, as if for an embrace.

9. With the assistance of the Group, ☼ picks up ☽, rocks her, then sets her on the ground, on hands and knees.

10. Group begins to walk in a cluster, circling the space, all talking at the same time again ignoring ☽, who crawls after them.

11. When ☽ is ready, she shrieks or calls, demanding attention. A member of the Group helps her to standing and she joins the Group.

12. Group continues to walk for a few steps as a tight group, conversing, then Breaks into silence and different directions.

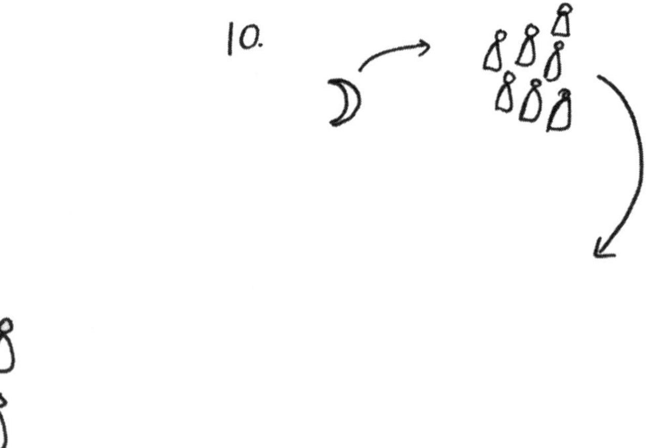

Beading Ritual

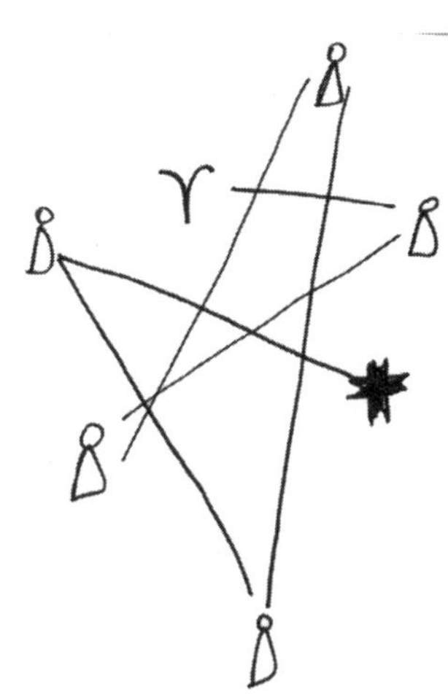

In this ritual, we bead as a community, to experience how we are connected and all contribute to a larger pattern of creation. Women can share stories while beading, or the beading structure can frame the space for other rituals.

1. Group creates a shape in the space with the beading string — every member holds the string taut. ♈ is at the head of the string, ✱ is at the end of the spool.

2. ♈ beads. As she beads, other members alternately kneel and stand to allow the bead to travel from one member to the next.

3. Every five to 10 beads, ♈ hands off the beading role to another member of the group, ✱ hands off the ending role to another member of the group, the group changes its physical configuration.

4. Repeat.

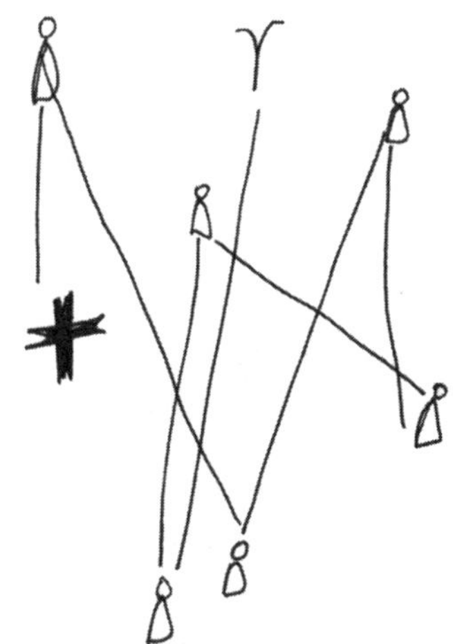

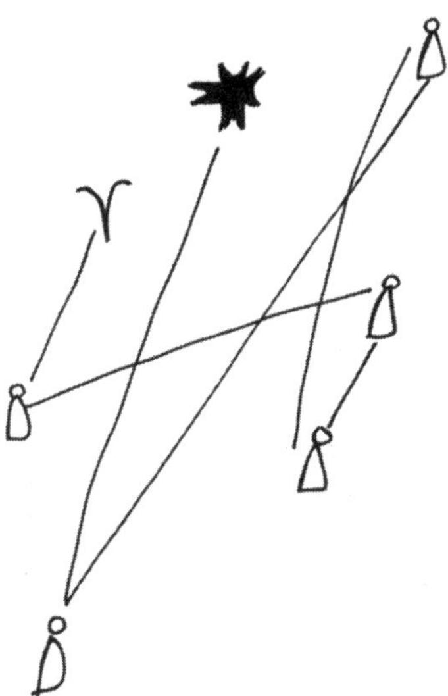

Rituals of Female Friendship

The theory of pre-patriarchal matriarchal societies comes from 19th century anthropologists. It was immediately and enthusiastically taken up by first wave suffragists (including Elizabeth Cady Stanton, who wrote about it in her 1891 essay "The Matriarchate, or Mother-Age").

In her feminist historical-revisionist The Double Goddess: Women Sharing Power *from 2003, Vicki Noble tracks the reiterating figure of the double goddess in ancient artifacts as proof of a matriarchal system, one in which women ruled societies in pairs.*

Is this actually true? Who knows?

Who cares? To me, the idea of women running societies in pairs explains the particular intensity of female friendships: in their passionate closeness, the specificity of sharing lived experience, the close observation of others (socially denigrated as "gossip"). These relationships rehearse the roles women are meant to take — as leaders of society.

Friendship 1.
Babyhood: Parallel Play to Cooperative Play

Babies don't play with each other, they play next to each other. This is called "parallel play": toddlers learn through the exploration of their own bodies in their environment, while also having their play partly stimulated and then directed by absorbing the play of the other children around them.

In celebration of this initiatory phase of female friendship, participants, in pairs, engage in parallel play until their play organically reaches some form of cooperation.

Friendship 2.
Girlhood: Mirroring to Routines

We are now at early girlhood. Participants, in pairs, engage in mirroring play and early routines. Laughter is welcome throughout.

1. In pairs, women spin, holding each other's hands or wrists. They crouch on the ground, arms draped behind each other's backs.

2. Pair stands, and with their inner arms connected, reach up to the sky and then bow down to the ground.

3. Pair walks themselves to the floor, lying down on their right side, facing the same direction, knees drawn in. Pair rolls onto their back — then onto their left side, onto their belly, onto their right side, then onto their belly.

4. From that position, pair begins a mirrored gestural rhythm, coming into sitting, then standing facing in the same direction, inner arms pressed into each other.

5. Pair runs across the room, then stops suddenly, facing one another, making a bridge with their arms. Repeats, again running across the room, then stopping suddenly making a bridge with their arms.

6. Pair moves into a simple routine dance with each other that takes them out of the space. This choreography can change depending on the group.

THE GHOSTS WE LIVE WITH

DODIE BELLAMY

Most ghosts are confused. They manifest pale and elongated. But some ghosts are professionals, spirits who use a medium to enter a circle of believers. They plunge their disembodied arms into hot wax, and the wax hardens to a hollow skin, capturing the shape of a thumb from beyond or a clawlike fist. Believers display these bits of dimensionality in glass-fronted cabinets. Ghosts flow through key holes, flicker behind the bathroom door while you splash in the tub. Ghosts sneak up from behind when you look in a mirror, where in its gloss you too waver about, flat and empty. Some ghosts have personalities and can even speak. They convey their emotions via smells the living recognize. Other ghosts manifest as vaporous fogs or cold swirling funnels. Some are fragments of disembodied drives, little glowing orbs that that zip about super fast.

An evolved ghost is called an entity. An entity knows what it wants and who to terrorize to get it. Flashes of a bramble-headed woman appear at the foot of your bed. Poltergeist means noisy ghost because it bangs things around. It lives inside your TV and rearranges the objects in your home in configurations that break the laws of gravity. At first you find its quirkiness charming, but eventually it slams you against the wall, hangs your body upside-down from the ceiling like a bat. You wake up in the middle of fucking and find yourself alone in bed, pummeled by this energy envelope that smells like rancid wax. Ghosts slain in battle are particularly persistent. To escape them, you must run around your village three times and wash yourself.

My building predates the 1906 earthquake, a humble Victorian built for workers. Its embossed walls are thick with residual ectoplasm from all the lives that have passed through these six units. We host a hungry ghost who moves from apartment to apartment, latching onto holes in the occupant's aura, forcing them to overindulge in alcohol drugs food or sex. The preppy guy in 18A is suddenly a major stoner, pasty with zits on his face. The guy next door with the wealthy Republican parents, goes from being a responsible citizen to a drunk who plays video games full volume, at all hours, explosions of guns and bombs rattling our shared living room wall. His family ships him back to Vermont for detox. His replacement is a drunk from the get-go, abandoning the apartment to druggy friends. I peek through their open front door and see a maze of filth, like the contents of more than one apartment have fused and are stacked in a double layer. The handsome rocker guy I've lived above for years suddenly becomes a junkie. When his drugs are delivered, I see him in front of our building, in sweatpants, shaky and thin, walking with a cane, sucking a red-white-and-blue rocket-shaped popsicle. He stops paying rent, is evicted, and his friends ship him back to Los Angeles for detox. After he leaves, I feel this presence wavering in the doorway, waiting. I start eating like there is no tomorrow, and now I'm fat because of the Minna Street ghost.

My back-porch office starts to rock and shake, making me queasy. It's not an earthquake. It's not a poltergeist. It's the alcoholic skateboarder who's moved in, a foot and a half beneath my floorboards, fucking in his illegal loft bed. Demons are making him fuck, the same demons that live inside my computer, demons who compel me to binge on information. I press the search button over and over and information streams through my eyes and into my body, so much information it's impossible to retain any particular bit of it. Online information, like avant-garde poetry or music, is a process, an onrush you experience moment by moment by moment, with no catchy tune, no overarching meaning, to pull it all together. It's not substances ghosts are hungry for, but time — a metronomic immersion to break the vast gray vague of eternity. Out of glowing screens they reach, lusting for time.

CONTRIBUTORS

Kristen Arnett is a queer fiction and essay writer. She was awarded *Ninth Letter*'s 2015 Literary Award in Fiction, was runner-up for the 2016 Robert Watson Literary Prize at *The Greensboro Review,* and was a finalist for *Indiana Review's* 2016 Fiction Prize. She's a columnist for *Literary Hub* and her work has appeared or is upcoming at *North American Review, The Normal School, Gulf Coast, TriQuarterly, Guernica, Electric Literature, McSweeneys, PBS Newshour, Literary Hub, Volume 1 Brooklyn,* OSU's *The Journal, Catapult, Bennington Review, Portland Review, Tin House* Flash Fridays/*The Guardian, Salon, The Rumpus*, and elsewhere. Her debut story collection, *Felt in the Jaw*, was published by Split Lip Press and was awarded the 2017 Coil Book Award. Her most recent novel is *Mostly Dead Things* (Tin House Books).

Dodie Bellamy is a novelist, poet, and essayist. She is the author of many books, including *When the Sick Rule the World, TV Sutras, Cunt Norton* and *Cunt-Ups.*

William Brewer is the author of *I Know Your Kind* (Milkweed Editions, 2017), a winner of the National Poetry Series, and *Oxyana*, which was selected for the Poetry Society of America's 30 and Under Chapbook Fellowship. His work has appeared in *American Poetry Review, New England Review, The New Yorker, A Public Space, The Sewanee Review,* and other journals. Formerly a Stegner Fellow, he is currently a Jones Lecturer at Stanford University.

Kathryn Davis is the author of eight novels, the most recent of which is *The Silk Road* (2019). Her other books are *Labrador* (1988), *The Girl Who Trod on a Loaf* (1993), *Hell: A Novel* (1998), *The Walking Tour* (1999), *Versailles* (2002), *The Thin Place* (2006) and *Duplex* (2013). She has received a Kafka Prize for fiction by an American woman, both the Morton Dauwen Zabel Award and the Katherine Anne Porter Award from the American Academy of Arts and Letters, and a Guggenheim Fellowship. In 2006, she won the Lannan Foundation Literary Award. She is the senior fiction writer on the faculty of The Writing Program at Washington University.

Colin Dickey is the author of *Ghostland: An American History in Haunted Places*, along with two other books of nonfiction. He is currently writing a book on conspiracy theories and other delusions, *The Unidentified*, forthcoming in 2020.

Fernando A. Flores is the author of *Death to the Bullshit Artists of South Texas* and the novel *Tears of the Trufflepig.* He lives in Austin.

Maya Gurantz works in video, performance, installation, social practice, and writing. Selected recent shows include (solo) the Museum of Contemporary Art Denver, the Grand Central Art Center, Greenleaf Gallery, Pieter PASD, (group) the Museum of Contemporary Art Utah, the Oakland Museum of California, Beaconsfield Gallery Vauxhall, Art Center College of Design, The Goat Farm Atlanta, The Great Wall of Oakland, High Desert Test Sites, and Movement Research at Judson Church. She recently received the inaugural Pieter Performance Grant for Dancemakers. She has written for *This American Life, The Frame* on KPCC, *The Awl, Notes on Looking, Avidly,* the *Los Angeles Review of Books, Acid-Free, Baumtest Quarterly,* and *RECAPS Magazine,* and co-hosts *The Sauce*, a podcast that dissects the intersections of culture and politics.

Brenda Hillman is the author of ten collections of poetry: *White Dress, Fortress, Death Tractates, Bright Existence, Loose Sugar, Cascadia, Pieces of Air in the Epic, Practical Water*, for which she won the LA Times Book Award for Poetry, *Seasonal Works with Letters on Fire,*which received the 2014 Griffin Poetry Prize and the Northern California Book Award for Poetry; and her most recent *Extra Hidden Life, Among the Days.* In 2016 she was named Academy of American Poets Chancellor. Among other awards Hillman has received are the 2012 Academy of American Poets Fellowship, the 2005 William Carlos Williams Prize for poetry, and Fellowships from the National Endowment for the Arts and the Guggenheim Foundation

Elisabeth Houston is a poet and playwright. She teaches in the English Department at Cal-State Los Angeles.

Anna Journey is the author of the essay collection *An Arrangement of Skin* (Counterpoint, 2017) and three books of poems: *The Atheist Wore Goat Silk* (LSU Press, 2017), *Vulgar Remedies* (LSU Press, 2013), and *If Birds Gather Your Hair for Nesting* (University of Georgia Press, 2009), which was selected by Thomas Lux for the National Poetry Series. She is an assistant professor of English at the University of Southern California.

Paul La Farge is the author of *The Night Ocean* (2017) and three other novels; also a book of imaginary dreams, *The Facts of Winter*. He lives in upstate New York.

Anna Merlan is a senior reporter at Gizmodo Media Group's Special Projects Desk. Her book, *Republic of Lies: American Conspiracy Theories and Their Surprising Rise to Power,* is out now from Metropolitan Books. She lives in New York.

Adam Morris is the author of *American Messiahs: False Prophets of a Damned Nation* (Liveright, 2019).

Matt Morton is the author of *Improvisation without Accompaniment*, winner of the 2018 A. Poulin, Jr. Poetry Prize, forthcoming from BOA Editions. His poetry has appeared in *AGNI*, *Gettysburg Review*, *Harvard Review*, *Tin House Online*, and elsewhere. His work has received support from the National Endowment for the Arts, the Bread Loaf Writers' Conference, the Sewanee Writers' Conference, the Johns Hopkins University Writing Seminars, and the University of North Texas, where he is a Robert B. Toulouse Doctoral Fellow in English.

Sarah Moss is the author of six novels, a memoir and some essays. Her latest book, *Ghost Wall,* is longlisted for the Women's Prize and shortlisted for the Royal Society of Literature Ondaatje Prize. She lives in the English West Midlands, where she is Professor of Creative Writing at the University of Warwick.

Masande Ntshanga is the author of the novels *The Reactive* and *Triangulum*. He is the winner of the Betty Trask Award in 2018, the inaugural PEN International New Voices Award in 2013, and a finalist for the Caine Prize in 2015. His work has appeared in *The White Review*, *Berlin Quarterly*, *Chimurenga*, *VICE*, *n+1*, and *Rolling Stone Magazine.*

Emily Ogden is the author of *Credulity: A Cultural History of US Mesmerism* (University of Chicago Press, 2018). She has written for the *New York Times, Critical Inquiry, Lapham's Quarterly Online, The Immanent Frame, American Literature, J19, Public Books,* and *Early American Literature*. Her regular column appears at *3 Quarks Daily.*

Zoe Tuck was born in Texas, became a person in California, and now lives in Massachusetts, where she is building the Threshold Academy, a bookstore and non-traditional educational/performance space. She co-curates the But Also house reading series. Zoe is the author of *Terror Matrix* (Timeless, Infinite Light 2014), and is currently working on new poems and a critical book of trans poetics.

Vanessa Angélica Villarreal was born in the Rio Grande Valley borderlands to formerly undocumented Mexican immigrants. She is the author of the collection *Beast Meridian* (Noemi Press, Akrilica Series, 2017), a Kate Tufts Discovery Award finalist and winner of the John A. Robertson Award for Best First Book of Poetry from the Texas Institute of Letters. Her work has been featured in *BuzzFeed*, the *Academy of American Poets* Poem-a-Day, *The Boston Review*, *The Rumpus*, the *Los Angeles Times*, *NBC News*, and elsewhere. She is a CantoMundo Fellow and is currently pursuing her doctorate in English Literature and Creative Writing at the University of Southern California in Los Angeles, where she is raising her son with the help of a loyal dog.

Keziah Weir is an associate editor at *Vanity Fair.*

Aaron Winslow writes fiction, criticism, video games, and screenplays. His recent work has appeared in the *Los Angeles Review of Books*, *Social Text Online*, and *Full Stop*, among other places. His science fiction novel, *Jobs of the Great Misery*, is available from Skeleton Man Press. He teaches writing at the University of Southern California. Further information and writing can be found at aaron-winslow.com.

Javier Zamora was born in El Salvador and migrated to the US when he was nine. He is a Radcliffe Fellow at Harvard University. Zamora's poetry and prose appear in *Granta, The Kenyon Review, Poetry, The New York Times,* and elsewhere. *Unaccompanied,* Copper Canyon Press, is his first collection.

FEATURED ARTISTS

Reza Shafahi (b.1940, Iran) is a self-taught artist who first started painting in 2012, at the ripe age of 72. As part of a long-term art project, Daddy Sperm, by his son Mamali Shafahi, both father and son worked on identical subjects and showed them side-by-side in the Daddy Sperm exhibition in Paris. Since then, Reza Shafahi has continued drawing from his own imagination and with his own inspiration.

His work has been exhibited in Magic of Persia (Dubai), Marlborough Chelsea Gallery, New York, SpazioA Gallery in Pistoia and the Erratum Galerie, Berlin. Novels, Khayyam poems, cinema, television, photographs and world news have had a great influence on the formation of his works, but what is actually seen by the viewer seems far removed from the world, and instead seems to encapsulate a hidden life of fantasy and dark eroticism. In 2019 he will be part of "City Prince/sses" at the Palais de Tokyo in Paris.

Kenneth Anger, an underground filmmaker and Hollywood enfant terrible, has been purveyor of shock and awe in a career that has spanned seven decades. Working

FEATURED ARTISTS

primarily in the format of the short film, Anger has merged Surrealism with his own brand of homoeroticism, suffused with violence and the supernatural. Influenced by the teachings of British occultist Aleister Crowley, Anger has searched for ever more transgressive subjects; from homosexual gang rape to Nazi propaganda footage and exploding airships. An avid self-mythologiser, his Hollywood career started as a child actor, and in his teens he began to work on his own films. His collage technique makes use of dramatic jump cuts and popular music soundtracks, but the gritty, experimental content meant he was often on the receiving end of societal outrage. He also authored salacious biographies of Hollywood from the silent film era up to the 1950s, exposing their sleazy sex lives and taste in narcotics. In recent years, Anger's archive of Hollywood memorabilia has been exhibited as an art installation, ushering in a wave of appreciation for his oeuvre from a younger generation.

Ana Mendieta was born in Havana, Cuba, in 1948, and died in New York City in 1985. She created groundbreaking work in photography, film, video, drawing, sculpture, and site-specific installations in a brief yet prolific career. Among the major themes in her work are exile, displacement, and a return to the landscape, which remain profoundly relevant today. Her unique hybrid of form and documentation, works that she titled "siluetas," are fugitive and potent traces of the artist's inscription of her body in the landscape, often transformed by natural elements such as fire and water.

The Estate of Ana Mendieta Collection, LLC, in collaboration with Galerie Lelong & Co., recently catalogued and digitized the entirety of Mendieta's moving image works, discovering that the artist remarkably made more than 100 in the ten-year period in which she worked in the medium. The groundbreaking exhibition of her moving image works, Covered in Time and History: The Films of Ana Mendieta, was organized by the Katherine E. Nash Gallery, University of Minnesota in 2014, and has since travelled to several institutions worldwide, including NSU Art Museum Fort Lauderdale, Florida; University of California, Berkeley Art Museum and Pacific Film Archive; Bildmuseet, Umeå, Sweden; Martin Gropius Bau, Berlin; and the Galerie nationale du Jeu de Paume, Paris.

Susan Cianciolo (b. 1969) lives and works in New York and from 1995-2001, she produced her critically acclaimed collection "RUN," aspects of which have reappeared in recent performances and installations. Her works have been featured in the 2017 Whitney Biennial at the Whitney Museum of American Art in New York, and has been included in group exhibitions at Akademie der Kunst in Berlin, MoMA PS1 in New York, the Swiss Institute in New York, Interstate Projects in Brooklyn, White Columns in New York, and Portikus in Frankfurt. Many of her solo exhibitions have been organized by Yale Union in Portland, Bridget Donahue in New York, Modern Art in London, 356 Mission in Los Angeles, and Alleged Gallery in New York. The artist studied Fashion Design at Parsons New School for Design, and painting at Winchester School of Art in the UK. Cianciolo is currently a professor at The Pratt Institute in New York.

Raha Raissnia (b. 1968, Tehran, Iran) lives and works in Brooklyn, New York. Her densely textured paintings, drawings, and films rely in equal measure on the gestural and photographic, the figurative and abstract. Both her films and two-dimensional work render these boundaries ambiguous through layers of manipulation and reference, generating contrapuntal compositions through the imbrication and excavation of images. Raissnia's work has been the subject of one-person and group exhibitions at the Museum of Modern Art (New York), The Drawing Center (New York), Ab/Anbar Gallery (Tehran), White Columns (New York), Galerie Xippas (Paris), Isfahan Museum of Contemporary Art (Isfahan, Iran), and the 56th Venice Biennale, among other places. Her interest in avant-garde filmmaking led her to work at Anthology Film Archives, where she has also exhibited. Raissnia's projection-performances, often undertaken in collaboration with Aki Onda and Panagiotis Mavridis, have been held at venues including the Whitney Museum of American Art (New York), REDCAT (Los Angeles), Kunsthal Rotterdam, Arnolfini – Center for Contemporary Arts (Bristol, UK), and Issue Project Room (New York). Raissnia's sixth one-person exhibition at Miguel Abreu Gallery was on display in the winter of 2019.

Vivan Sundaram was born in 1943 in Shimla, India and based in New Delhi, Sundaram was trained as a painter at M.S. University of Baroda and at the Slade School of Fine Art in London in the 1960s; he returned to India in 1970 and began a series of solo and group exhibitions; from 1990, he began to move towards sculpture, installation, and photography, and video. His work has been widely exhibited in India and in several international biennials. He has had solo shows in many cities of India as well as in New York, Chicago, London, Paris, Toronto, Montreal and Copenhagen. Sundaram is a founding member and trustee of the Sahmat collective. He lives in Delhi and is married to the art critic, curator and theorist, Geeta Kapur.